A Compendium of Useful Information from the Past for the Home, Garden and Household

◆ ◆ ◆

·EDITED BY DONALD J. BERG·

Ten Speed Press

TEN SPEED PRESS
P.O. Box 7123
Berkeley, CA 94707

Library of Congress Cataloging-in-Publication Data

Berg, Donald.
  Homestead hints.

  Includes index.
  1. Gardening—Miscellanea. 2. Home economics—Miscellanea. 3. Do-it-yourself work—Miscellanea.
I. Title
SB453.B418   1986   640   86-40334
ISBN 0-89815-181-3 (pbk.)

Book and cover design by ANTIQUITY REPRINTS
Type set by John Moses/Modular Compart Graphics

Printed in the United States of America
1 2 3 4 5 — 90 89 88 87 86

3

Foreword

◆ ◆ ◆ ◆ ◆

You've probably let your homestead get a bit run down. Nature's elements are working against you every minute. With a little bit of time that you can spare for work around the house, you need all the help you can get. You need this book!

All of the advice that you'll find has been hidden away on the pages of old farm journals, home and garden magazines and household guide books since the last century. Back then, without today's time-saving technology, it was much more important to find the most efficient way of doing things. People depended on these hints to get their work done well.

Don't expect to be able to use all of the advice. Not all of us have to remove boulders from the garden or chase birds from the orchard, but I hope that you'll find a few hints that will make your life a little bit easier. — Donald J. Berg

CONTENTS

• • ◆ • •

• • ◆ • •

Farmer Snug's Residence

Farmer Slack's Place

Hints for the Homestead

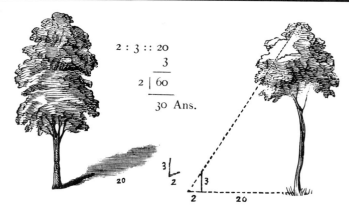

$$2 : 3 :: 20$$
$$3$$
$$2\ |\ 60$$
$$30\ \text{Ans.}$$

How to Find the Height of Trees

From an issue of VICK'S MONTHLY MAGAZINE from the 1880s

The height of a tree may be estimated sufficiently exact for ordinary purposes by the following method:

Being in the neighborhood of a tree, the height of which you wish to know, and in your hand you carry a walking cane, or a jointed fishing rod, and supposing the cane, or a length of the rod, is three feet, set it in the ground perpendicularly and, if the sun shines, it will cast a shadow; now, with a pocket rule, you measure the length of the shadow, and find it, say two feet. Here, then, we have a right angle of two feet and three feet. Now, supposing the tree to be tolerably straight, measure from its base to the end of its shadow, and we will suppose it to be twenty feet. Now, if a cane three feet high casts a shadow of two feet, how high must a tree be to cast a shadow of twenty feet? Or, in other words, if two gives three, how much twenty feet give?

But suppose the sun don't shine, what then? Why, then set up the cane as before, say eighteen feet from the base of the tree. Now, place your head on the ground, with the cane between you and the tree, moving nearer to or further from it, until you can just see the top of the tree over the top of the cane; place a pebble or mark on the ground at the point where you obtain this view. The cane being three feet high, the distance from the pebble to it will be two feet; hence, by the same rule, we ascertain the height of the tree to be thirty feet.

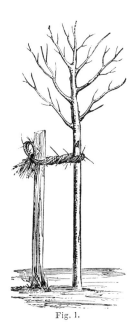

Fig. 1.

Fig. 2.

Staking Trees

◆ ◆ ◆ ◆ ◆

From THE AMERICAN AGRICULTURIST, 1866

When young trees have the proper balance of root and top, there is seldom need of staking them except in very exposed places. But there are cases in which it is necessary to do it, especially where large trees are moved. Two firm stakes are placed opposite each other in the direction of the prevailing winds, and about a foot from the trunk of the tree, or one stake only may be used. The figures show two methods of securing the tree. In figure 1, a straw rope is put around the tree, twisted until it reaches the stake, and then passed around it, and fastened by a nail. In fig. 2, the tree is kept in place by two straps of leather or stout canvas, which are secured to the stakes by nails.

Plant Sugar Maples

From THE FARMER'S & EMIGRANT'S HAND BOOK, 1845

All good citizens, who are desirous of doing good deeds, and of being remembered by posterity hereafter, we would recommend to transplant a goodly number of sugar maples round their dwellings. We think all will see the propriety of giving their immediate attention to the growing of this most valuable tree, not only for adorning our dewellings, but also, a large number may be set in a suitable place on every farm. They, in a few years, will afford the pure juice for sugar, and the best of timber for cabinet and other kinds of work, and all poor trees may be worked up for fuel. Our soil is rich and well adapted for the sugar maple.

This tree, beside or around a dwelling is an ornament, and also by the road-side. How pleasant and beautiful would be the scenery, if this tree, in its full growth and splendor, were along each side of our roads! We have seen the maple tree no taller than a walking-staff, become, in fifteen years, so large as to afford sap and sugar. Be not discouraged by looking forward, and say it will be a long time before you can have any benefit by sugar. You must remember the timber is growing every year, and wait with patience, and be assured the other part will not fail.

Hints to Wood Cutters

◆ ◆ ◆ ◆ ◆

From THE REGISTER OF RURAL AFFAITS, 1860 and 1866

PILING CORD WOOD — In piling cord wood place the bark side upward, as it will then turn off the water, keeping the wood dryer, and preventing the bark from dropping off and being lost when it is moved.

◆ ◆ ◆ ◆ ◆

Most kinds of wood cut in winter, and left in large logs in the woods, becomes more or less soured and injured. If wood could be cut and split in summer, when the weather would dry it rapidly, the wood would be greatly increased in value; but as this is usually impracticable, the next best is to cut and split it in winter as fine as will be required, and then cord it up in a wood-house, well sheltered from rains, but admitting the free circulation of the air.

Useful Contrivances

From the book HOMEMADE CONTRIVANCES, 1899

A handy arrangement for hanging up articles, as for instance, tools in the shop, or meats and other eatables in the storeroom, is shown in the accompanying sketch. This plan is particularly to be commended where it is desired to get the articles up out of the reach of mice, rats or cats. Suspend a worn-out buggy wheel to the ceiling by an iron bolt, with a screw thread on one end and a nut or head upon the other. The wheel can be hung as high or as low as desired. Hooks can be placed all about the rim and upon the spokes, in the manner shown, giving room in a small space for the hanging up of a great many articles. This arrangement is convenient, also, from the fact that one can swing the wheel about and bring all articles within reach without moving.

♦ ♦ ♦ ♦ ♦

From THE REGISTER OF RURAL AFFAIRS, 1868

Ladders are nearly always made with blunt, rounded, or square ends; and as a consequence, when placed upon a smooth surface, especially if frozen or icy, there is danger of their slipping or falling. The lower ends should always be sharp or wedge form. If much used, they should be shod with iron—the simplest mode of doing which, is to take an iron strap, bend it, by heating in the fire or forge, to a sharp angle in the middle, so as to fit the wedge form of the feet, and then nail it on through holes punched for the purpose.

A Partner in the Wood Pile

❖ ❖ ❖ ❖ ❖

From THE RURAL NEW YORKER, 1894

Three stakes, two nine and the other 10 feet long, are nailed together as shown in the picture, making a three-cornered frame on which swings a wooden pendulum eight feet long. There are holes in it so that it can swing at different lengths, on a bolt at the upper part of the frame. Two boards on the frame guide the rod. With the end of the saw fastened to the lower end of the swing rod, you have about the motion given by another man. We believe that we could do better work with this than with a partner who persisted in "riding the saw." Some of our readers who have tried this plan, speak highly of it.

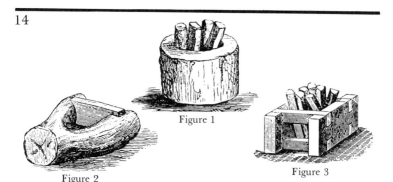

Figure 1

Figure 2

Figure 3

Splitting Wood

♦ ♦ ♦ ♦ ♦

From THE REGISTER OF RURAL AFFAIRS, 1873

In large portions of the country, farmers still burn wood as a fuel, and some of them consume much time needlessly in splitting it for the stove, being compelled to stoop at every blow of the axe and pick up sticks by hand. The accompanying figure (fig. 1) represents a very simple contrivance for holding each block after it has been sawed, until by successive blows of the axe the whole is reduced to small pieces, without the necessity of stooping over to pick up each stick separately. In the absence of a hollow log, from which it is made, the jack or wood-holder may be constructed in other ways, one of which is to select a forked log, and set in a thick piece across, as shown in fig. 2. The space in the fork may be cut out larger, so as to give the opening a rounder form. Fig. 3 shows one made of thick plank or flat timber, in a more compact shape, the two side-pieces being secured together at the top and bottom by short pieces of stout scantling halved or dovetailed into them, and spiked in their places. A simple jack of this kind may last several years, and save many days' work every winter to the farmer who saws and splits short wood, and who, in addition to keeping the cooking stove in operation the year round, has one or two other fires for heating rooms during winter. It will be observed, in constructing these contrivances, that they must be heavy and solid, so as to keep their places, and not to be thrown about while in use, and to be firm enough to withstand the heavy blows to which they will be occasionally subjected.

A Portable Wood·box

♦ ♦ ♦ ♦ ♦

From THE AMERICAN AGRICULTURIST, 1878

In many localities, even in mid-summer, there are cool spells, in which a little fire in the evening is necessary, not only for comfort, but for health. Those who, with the approach of warm weather, put away all the fire-making appliances, may find a folding wood-box, one which may be used when needed, and set aside when not wanted, a useful household contrivance. The box referred to is shown in the engraving, and may be of a size suited to the wood need, and the quantity it is required to hold. It consists of a frame made of slabs of pine, or other convenient wood, an inch and a quarter thick, hinged together with a wooden pin, or by carriage bolts. The sides and ends are made of any heavy canvas or bagging, tacked to the frame, as shown in the engraving. If desired, the wood-box may be ornamented by the use of brass, or other bright-headed tacks, and the working of a monogram or initial letter on the sides and ends with some bright colored worsted. Such a wood-box will keep "dirt" from the floor, and when the time for which it is required has passed, it can be so folded as to occupy but a small space until a change in the weather to cooler may call it into use again.

Carrying FireWood

From THE AMERICAN AGRICULTURIST, 1883

The accompanying engraving shows two convenient methods of carrying fire wood. A wood rack for the shoulder is made of a piece of round hardwood, with four long pins set in the upper side. These pins are placed in V-shaped pairs, between which the fire wood is piled. A handle, three feet long, is set in a hole bored in the centre of the under side of the body of the rack. This device, when complete, resembles a "skeleton" hod, and is carried in the same manner as a hod for brick or mortar. A second method of carrying wood consists of a stout canvas "apron," in the lower part of which the fuel is placed, as shown in the engraving. A boy, or other person, with much wood to move short distances, will find either of these methods labor-saving, and they are quickly made.

17

A Martin Box

From THE NATIONAL FARMER'S & HOUSEKEEPER'S CYCLOPEDIA, 1888
♦ ♦ ♦

The box-house does very well if made of any small box about fifteen inches square with a division put in it so that two families can inhabit it. A square hole should be sawed out at the bottom edge opposite each division, and the bottom nailed on. Place the box on a pole from twelve to fifteen feet high, or on the gable end of a roof, or even in a tree, and your house is finished. It can be painted or not, or even made in fancy designs, which are quite attractive to the eye. The illustration given on this page will convey the idea. A hop, or other rapid-growing climber, if planted at the bottom of the pole, will climb up it and cause it to look quite ornamental and picturesque. We have seen them built two stories high, made like a diminutive gothic cottage, which is quite pretty. The house should be made before the martins come, as they are generally in a hurry to locate and go to "housekeeping." By all means give them some kind of a home.

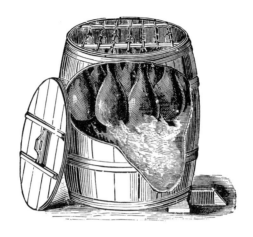

A Simple Smoke House

From the book BARN PLANS AND OUTBUILDINGS, 1884

◆ ◆ ◆ ◆ ◆

It sometimes happens that one needs to smoke some hams or other meat, and no smoke house is at hand. In such a case a large cask or barrel, as shown may prove a very good substitute. To make this effective, a small pit should be dug, and a flat stone or a brick placed across it, upon which the edge of the cask will rest. Half of the pit is beneath the barrel, and half of it outside. The head and bottom may be removed, or a hole can be cut in the bottom a little larger than the portion of the pit beneath the cask. The head is removed while the hams are hung upon cross stocks. These rest upon two cross-bars, made to pass through holes bored in the sides of the cask, near the top. The head is then laid upon the cask, and covered with sacks to confine the smoke. Some coals are put into the pit outside of the cask, and the fire is fed with damp corn cobs, hardwood chips, or fine brush. The pit is covered with a flat stone, by which the fire may be regulated, and it is removed when necessary to add more fuel.

Hints on Home Heating

From PRACTICAL HOUSEKEEPING, 1883

TO START A FIRE IN DAMP, STILL WEATHER – Light a few bits of shavings or paper placed upon the top of grate; thus by the heated air's forcing itself into the chimney and establishing there an upward current, the room is kept free from the gas and smoke which is so apt to fill it, and the fire can then be lighted from below with good success.

◆

TO REMOVE RUST FROM A STOVEPIPE – Rub with linseed oil (a little goes a great way); build a slow fire till it is dry. Oil in the Spring to prevent it from rusting.

◆

COAL FIRE – If your coal fire is low, throw on a tablespoon of salt and it will help it very much.

◆

TIME TO CUT TIMBER – Hard wood for timber or fire-wood whould be cut in August, September or October. Hoop-poles should be cut before frost comes; cut at other times, there is danger of worms.

◆

WHEN A CHIMNEY TAKES FIRE—throw salt on the fire, and shut off the draught as much as possible, and it will burn out slowly.

STUMP BORED FOR BURNING.

Useful Information

¹ From THE NATIONAL FARMER'S & HOUSEKEEPER'S CYCLOPEDIA, 1888

BURNING STUMPS — Tree stumps are said to be easily removed by boring a two-inch hole eighteen inches deep into the stump. Do this in the fall, and fill with a concentrated solution of saltpetre, and plug up to keep out water. By spring it will have permeated every part. Then fill the hole with kerosene, set on fire, and the whole stump, it is said, will be consumed, even to the roots. It would seem to be feasible, and it is certainly an easy way to get rid of stumps. The ashes will remain to fertilize the soil.

◆ ◆ ◆

From the book THE AMERICAN WOMAN'S HOME, 1869

A Shallow fireplace saves wood and gives out more heat than a deeper one. A false back of brick may be put up in a deep fireplace. Hooks for holding up the shovel and tongs, a hearth-brush and bellows, and brass knobs to hang them on, should be furnished to every fireplace. An iron bar across the andirons aids in keeping the fire safe and in good order.

◆ ◆ ◆

From THE UNIVERSAL RECEIPT BOOK, 1831

From a knowledge of the velocity with which sound travels, the distance of a thunder-cloud may be very accurately deduced. The period of time between seeing the lightning and hearing the thunder must be taken, and if a stop-watch, or pendulum, is not at hand, the pulse may be used; for the pulsations of a healthy adult approach so near to seconds, that in the time of four or five of them no very sensible error can arise. Multiply the number by 1142 feet, the distance through which sound moves in a second.

Living Fence Posts

From THE AMERICAN AGRICULTURIST, 1867

To make rail fences comparatively permanent, you must have self-supporting stakes, that is, stakes that will firmly support themselves, and also the weight of the fence and waters. To make a stake self-supporting, it must have roots to enable it to retain a firm hold of the earth. The willow, white, or yellow, is for this purpose about as near being "the right thing in the right place," as any tree we can find. It grows without trouble, and is a natural denizen of wet, marshy grounds; therefore it is well adapted for stakes through bottom lands. The stakes may be cut from three to ten feet in length, and from three inches to a foot in diameter. They may be set in holes made with a post auger, about two feet deep, firmly ramming the earth around them; or they may be pointed, and driven into the ground. In one season they will be well rooted, thrifty trees, well able to resist, and hold the fence against, the impetuosity of the rushing water.

The willow grows easily from cuttings, and when properly pruned, makes a beautiful tree. From its rapid growth it is rendered valuable as a shade tree for pasture lands. It grows almost as well on the hill top as in the valley, unless the former be very dry or rocky.

How to Work with Glass

From the book THE FARMER'S NEW GUIDE, 1893

HOW TO CUT GLASS — It is not generally known that glass may be cut, under water, with a strong pair of scissors. If a round or oval be required, take a piece of common window-glass, draw the shape upon it in a black line; sink it with your left hand under water as deep as you can without interfering with the view of the line, and with your right use the scissors to cut away what is not required.

TO BORE HOLES IN GLASS — Any sharp steel will cut glass with great facility when kept freely wet with camphor dissolved in turpentine. A drill may be used, or even the hand alone. A hole may be readily enlarged by a round file. The ragged edges of glass may also be thus smoothed with a flat file. Flat window glass can be readily sawed by a watch-spring saw, by the aid of this solution. In short, the most brittle glass can be wrought almost as easily as wood, by the use of drilling tools kept constantly moist with camphorized oil of turpentine.   ♦ ♦ ♦

From the book PRACTICAL HOUSEKEEPING, 1883

TO CUT GLASS JARS — Fill the jar with lard-oil to where you want to cut the jar; then heat an iron-rod or bar to red-heat; immerse in the oil; the unequal expansion will crack the jar all round at the surface of the oil, and you can lift off the top part.

Useful Contrivances

◆ ◆ ◆ ◆ ◆

A SIMPLE DEVICE FOR PICKING UP LEAVES consists of a sheet nailed on two opposite edges to heavy laths, as shown in the figure above. To use it, the cloth is laid upon a heap of leaves, the middle of each lath is grasped and the laths are then brought together under the heap, thus inclosing more than a sugar barrel solid full at each haul.

From THE RURAL NEW YORKER, 1894

◆ ◆ ◆ ◆ ◆

HOW TO CARRY A LADDER — "Farmer W." carried home a long ladder which he had borrowed, and which was supposed to require four men to carry it. He balanced the ladder upon his wheelbarrow and lashed the sides of it to the handles of the barrow; then taking the end of the ladder, he wheeled it along with comparative ease.

From THE AMERICAN AGRICULTURIST, 1874

Figure 1   Figure 2

Transplanting Evergreens

◆ ◆ ◆ ◆ ◆

From THE REGISTER OF RURAL AFFAIRS, 1860

WHEN YOUNG EVERGREENS have their branches spreading out, down to the surface of the ground, as all evergreens should to look well, it is often quite difficult to dig them up for transplanting, these spreading prostrate branches impeding the work of the spade. Again, when they are set out, the same difficulty occurs in placing them properly in the hole, and filling in the earth. Having recently had occasion to set out a large number from the nursery rows, we found the work could not only be much better done, but in about one-half the time, by drawing the lower branches upwards, pressing them against the tree, and securing them in this position by passing around and tying a cord, as shown in fig. 2, the common appearance of the tree being represented by fig. 1. The ease with which the operator could now work was remarkable. Nurserymen, who have many such trees to dig, would find it to their advantage to provide a number of small straps to buckle around the trees during the operation of removal.

How to Shovel

From THE REGISTER OF RURAL AFFAIRS, 1867

As shoveling is such laborious and fatiguing work, every laborer should aim to derive aid of all the mechanical advantages that may be available, for the purpose of rendering such labor less fatiguing. And the same is true when pitching compost. In order to work with a shovel, or manure fork with little fatigue, that part of the labor which requires the exercise of the most muscular force, should be performed with the tool operating like a lever.

The illustration herewith given represents a laborer shoveling with the handle of the shovel across one knee, which is the fulcrum, the weight being on the shovel, and the power, the hand near the end of the handle. By placing the handle across one knee, the shovel is driven into the material to be shoveled, but a forward motion of the body, which requires very little muscular force.—Then, by a downward thrust of the hand near the end of the handle, the weight is raised one foot or more, with the expenditure of a very limited amount of muscular force.

◆ ◆ ◆

A Door Holder

◆ ◆ ◆ ◆

From THE AMERICAN AGRICULTURIST, 1880

A simple apparatus for holding a swinging barndoor open at any point, was described to us in Livingston Co., N.Y. (We did not note down the name of the contriver—an aged farmer, who busies himself with making new devices for ordinary work.) This is a stick, 2 to 3 feet long, with an iron ring or thimble around the lower end, to prevent splitting. A sharpened iron rod of any desired length is driven in. The other end is supplied with a hook to catch into a staple driven into the door. When not in use, it is turned horizontally, and the lower end rests on a spike or wooden pin, as shown by the dotted line in the engraved sketch. A similar stick on the other side could be used, if it is desired to hold the door only partly open, instead of swinging it back against the side of the barn, or against a stray post or other object.

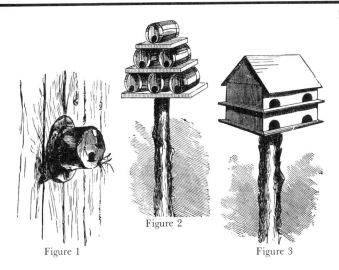

Figure 2

Figure 1   Figure 3

Bird Houses

◆ ◆ ◆ ◆ ◆

From the book BARN PLANS AND OUTBUILDINGS, 1884

It is a mistake to have bird houses too showy and too much exposed. Most birds naturally choose a retired place for their nests, and slip into them quietly, that no enemy may discover where they live. All that is required in a bird house is, a hiding place, with an opening just large enough for the bird, and a water-tight roof. There are so very many ways in which these may be provided, any boy can contrive to make all the bird houses that may be needed. An old hat, with a hole for a door, tacked by the rim against a shed, as in figure 1, will be occupied by birds sooner than a showy bird-house. Figure 2 shows how six kegs may be placed together to rest upon a pole; the kegs are fastened to the boards by screws inserted from beneath. Figure 3 shows how a two-story house may be made separate from two shallow boxes, each divided into four tenements. Each box has a bottom board, projecting two inches all around, to answer as a landing place. The roof should be tight, and the whole so strongly nailed that it will not warp. It should be well painted.

Wood Measure

From THE FARMERS' AND MECHANICS' MANUAL, 1869

TO ASCERTAIN THE CONTENTS OR NUMBER OF CORDS IN A GIVEN PILE OF WOOD — Multiply the length by the width, and that product by the height, which will give you the number of cubic feet. Divide that product by 128, and the quotient will be the number of cords.

A pile of wood 4 feet wide, and 4 feet high, and 8 feet long, contains 1 "cord"; and a "cord foot" is 1 foot in length of such a pile.

◆ ◆ ◆ ◆ ◆

TO ASCERTAIN THE CONTENTS (BOARD MEASURE) OF BOARDS, SCANTLING, AND PLANK — Multiply the breadth in inches by the thickness in inches, and that by the length in feet, and divide the product by 12, and the quotient will be the contents.

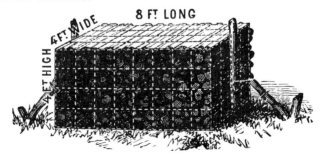

Useful Information
From THE REGISTER OF RURAL AFFAIRS, 1857

TO REMOVE OLD PUTTY, moisten it with muriatic acid, and it will immediately become soft.

♦ ♦ ♦

PAINTING HOUSES — The paint will harden better and last twice as long by being applied late in autumn, than during the hot season.

♦ ♦ ♦

BEE STINGS may be quickly cured by applying repeatedly a soft paste made of saleratus* and water— the potash neutralizes the acid poison.   *Baking Soda

♦ ♦ ♦

CRACKS IN STOVES may be effectually stopped by a paste made of ashes and salt, with water. Iron filings and sal ammoniac make a still harder and firmer cement.

♦ ♦ ♦

DURABILITY OF RED CEDAR — We have heard of an old farmer, who, when asked how he knew that cedar posts would "last forever," said he had frequently tried the experiment. Some may doubt his assertion, yet its lasting powers have been found to exceed a long lifetime. At the head of one of the graves in "Old St. Mary's," Md., there stands a cedar slab, which, as the inscription indicates, was placed there in 1717, and is still perfectly sound.

A Word to the Wise

From CENTURY MAGAZINE, 1885

◆ ◆ ◆ ◆ ◆

The great bugaboo of the birds is the owl. The owl snatches them from off their roosts at night, and gobbles up their eggs and young in their nests. He is a veritable ogre to them, and his presence fills them with consternation and alarm.

One season, to protect my early Cherries, I placed a large stuffed owl amid the branches of the tree. Such a racket as there instantly began about my grounds is not pleasant to think upon! The orioles and robins fairly "shrieked out their affright." The news instantly spread in every direction, and apparently every bird in town came to see that owl in the Cherry tree, and every bird took a Cherry, so that I lost more fruit than if I had left the owl indoors. With craning necks and horrified looks the birds would alight upon the branches, and between their screams would snatch off a Cherry, as if the act was some relief to their outraged feelings.

A Useful Contrivance

From THE AMERICAN AGRICULTURIST, 1866

Mr. G. B. Green, Hudson, N.Y., finding hand picking too slow, and wishing to avoid the stones and dirt that will be mixed with apples when gathered from the ground, contrived the device shown in the engraving. It consists of a spread made of stout burlap, 20 feet square, bound on the edges. In the center is a hole large enough to encircle the tree, and provided with a drawing string to fasten it to the trunk. From this hole is an opening to one side of the spread, to allow it to be put around the tree, and the opening is afterwards laced up by means of a string running through eyelet holes. In each of the corners of the spread a strong eyelet hole is worked—or what is better, an iron eye may be inserted. The spread being placed around the tree, three of the corners are raised up and stretched out by means of slender poles, in such a manner, that the corner without a pole will be the lowest. Under this depending corner is placed a barrel, or wagon if the tree be a tall one. The apples are shaken down on to the sheet, and roll towards the lower corner, where they are caught.

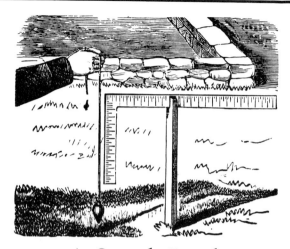

A Simple Level

From an issue of THE AMERICAN AGRICULTURIST from the 1880s

The accompanying engraving shows how easily a serviceable Level may be constructed with an ordinary carpenter's square, a short plumb-line, and a sharpened stake. The stake, with a split in the top, is driven into the ground, and the square adjusted as shown in the engraving. For the plumbline, a string and a piece of lead, or, in an emergency, even a stone, for the plummet, will answer. The line is fastened to the shorter arm of the square, so that it will run close to and parallel with the inner edge of the longer arm. As the two arms of the square are at right angles, when the longer one is perpendicular, as determined by the plumb-line, the shorter one is horizontal or level. Any objects sighted from *a*, along the upper edge to *b*, will be in the same plane, or on the same level.

Tell Time by the Sun

♦ ♦ ♦ ♦ ♦

From an issue of THE AMERICAN AGRICULTURIST from the 1870s

Good watches and clocks are common now-a-days, and there is no longer the use for sun dials and noon marks, which existed only a few years ago. Nevertheless, on farms a few miles from villages and town clocks, how often does it happen that the time is lost except as we depend upon the sun for it? At such times a sun dial is a real convenience, if it be large enough to give tolerably accurate time. Sun dials are always interesting, and may be made ornamental, and are certainly very appropriate ornaments to private or public grounds. In those of the ordinary form the gnomon or style which casts the shadow, is a right angle triangle, set with the long side up, to make the shadow. This long side should point directly toward the north pole. So that the north star, provided it could cast a visible shadow, (and indicated the exact north,) would cast none. To do this, the angle of elevation must be the same as the latitude of the place, and it must be set pointing due north.

Stone Fences

From THE AMERICAN AGRICULTURIST, 1867

In some regions a stone wall is the cheapest fence that can be made. In many respects, too, it is the best for farm purposes. It has a look of honest stability that is truly pleasing, but is rarely advisable, except where adjoining fields will furnish stones enough to inclose them, and the fields will be greatly improved by their removal. Every wall will tumble down some time or other. On springy soils, draining is indispensable. A trench should be dug a foot or more deep with plow and scraper. Then draw the larger stones for the foundation, and dump them in the trench, which will save much hand-lifting. Afterwards draw the smaller, scattering them along the entire line. Of course, the stones should be laid so as to bind as much as possible, and inclining inwards somewhat. If practical, find enough flat stones to cover the top of the fence, and help to throw off the rain, and to prevent Jack Frost from tearing it to pieces.

How to Carry a Watermelon
From THE AMERICAN AGRICULTURIST, 1878

We feel very sure that when a thing is needed, it will be supplied by some inventor. No one article in the market is more unmanageable than a watermelon. It is too large for the average basket, too troublesome to carry under the arm.

At all events, some genius has hit the popular want, and supplied what nature has failed to do: a handle, by which the watermelon can be as easily carried as any other parcel.

The essential part is the handle made of bass wood. This has a sufficient supply of strong twine, and two "beckets" of the same wood to distribute the pressure. When the melon is harnessed and ready for travel, it appears as in the figure.

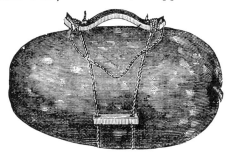

How to Remove Roof Snow
From THE AMERICAN AGRICULTURIST, 1875

In a heavy fall of snow, a sufficient quantity will collect upon a weak roof to break it down or force the rafters to spread and distort the shape of the building. Much damage occurs every winter by neglecting to clear roofs of snow immediately after a storm. A barn roof is not often accessible, nor is it safe or agreeable to stand upon the roof of a shed and shovel snow while a north-easter is blowing. We suggest the following plan of doing this work in a more comfortable fashion. A board 12 inches wide and 6 feet or less in length, is fastened to a long rope in the manner shown in the illustration. One end of the rope is thrown over the barn roof and held by a person on the rear side, who draws the board up on the roof until it reaches the peak. The person in front then draws the board down and scrapes the snow down with it. The board is then drawn up again, the person in front guiding it to the proper place with his end of the rope. The one in the rear steps along each time the board is drawn up a distance equal to its length, so as to bring the scraper in the proper position each time. To facilitate the drawing of the board up the roof, a short rope is temporarily fastened to its upper edge and to the long rope, by which it is made to lie flat as it is drawn up. The roofs should be cleared as soon as possible after each fall of snow.

Be Prepared for Winter

♦ ♦ ♦ ♦ ♦

From THE AMERICAN AGRICULTURIST, 1867

GUARD AGAINST FROSTS — It usually is the case that after the first few frosts we have a long succession of golden autumn days, just made for ripening fruit and bringing out the late blooming flowers. A very slight covering will protect a plant, and those who have a choice grape or tomato that is late in ripening, or Dahlias or other plants that are just in the height of their bloom, should have at hand some screen to protect them from the first frosts. A sheet or other cloth put up tentwise, or stretched in any way over the plant, will be all that is needed. In England the amateur fruit growers have regular fixtures, upon which a covering may be stretched when the trees are in flower, as well as when the fruit is ripening.

♦ ♦ ♦

From PARK'S FLORAL MAGAZINE, 1892

PROTECTION — After the ground has become frozen it will be well to furnish protection to the hardy roses, shrubs and bulbs. Clean straw placed around the plants a few inches deep does nicely for most kinds. The ever-bloomers should be pegged down and covered with straw before the ground gets a hard freeze. Lay some bricks or sticks over the straw, to keep the wind from blowing it away.

Figure 1 — The Common "SLEW"

Figure 2 — The "JUMPER"

Home·made Sleds

♦ ♦ ♦ ♦ ♦

From THE AMERICAN AGRICULTURIST, 1880

Figure 1 is the "slew" made of two barrel staves set a few inches apart and fastened by cross-pieces with a strip of board upon these, running lengthwise of the staves, and making the seat. The "slew" is a low, broad runner sled, which will go either end foremost, and (when the hill is icy) sideways as well as any way; hence its name.—The *Junper*, figure 2, is made of one stout stave, to which a bit of scantling one foot long is nailed, and upon the upper end of the scantling a board for a seat is fastened. This is not an easy thing to ride, as there is nothing to hold on to; and to a new hand, if the hill is steep, it is a *jumper* which will sometimes leave them behind.

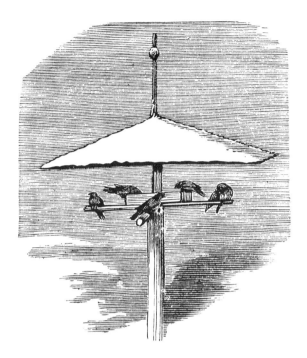

A Winter Feeder

From VICK'S MONTHLY MAGAZINE, 1880

♦ ♦ ♦ ♦ ♦

A neighbor who is a great observer of life out of doors, has already anticipated the wants of the birds, and proposes a Christmas present for them, similar to the accompanying sketch, which is simply a feed box and perches on top of a pole about four feet high, and a broad wood awning over all. He says: "The scraps from the table will be sufficient not only to give the birds a merry Christmas, but to keep them merry all through the winter, and I am sure that the life and gaiety of the birds about the house through the dull season will amply repay such a kindly investment."

How to Keep Rabbits and Mice from Barking

♦ ♦ ♦ ♦ ♦

From THE COUNTRY GENTLEMAN, 1855 and 1858

TO PREVENT RABBITS from barking young fruit trees, give the body of the young tree a thorough rubbing with soft soap. This not only prevents the rabbits from barking them, but it protects them against insects, takes all the rough scales off, softens the bark, and renders them much more thrifty that they would be otherwise. This simple recipe will be of vast value to the farmers in many parts of the West.—Greasing will prevent rabbits from barking fruit trees but it will also injure the tree.

♦ ♦ ♦ ♦ ♦

The *Granite Farmer* recommends stamping the snow hard round the body of fruit trees to prevent mice from girdling them. When the snow lays up light round the body of a tree, there is a cozy little place for mice to make their nests in the old grass around it. They do so. Soon hunger pinches, and rather than leave their warm cozy quarters they eat of the bark from the trees, and soon girdle them. Stamping the snow down about the trees, effectually covers up the grass around the trunks, the mice can get at nothing of which to make their nests, and they scamper off to more attractive quarters, leaving the trees untouched.

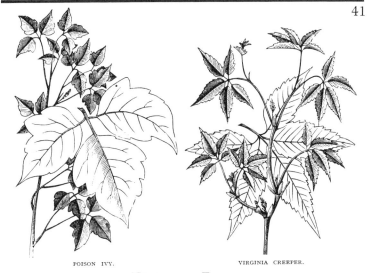

POISON IVY.   VIRGINIA CREEPER.

Poison Ivy

From the book PRACTICAL HOUSEKEEPING, 1883

POISON BY IVY — An infallible remedy for poisoning by ivy, poison oak and other poison vines and plants, is good rich butter milk in which you have beaten some green tansy leaves until the milk is thoroughly tinctured. Bathe the parts often (indeed, you could not do it too often,) until relieved. Wet a cloth with the mixture at night, and lay on, wetting as often as it feels dry.

HOW TO DETECT POISON IVY — The poison ivy and the innocuous kind differ in one particular which is too easy of remembrance to be overlooked by any one who is interested enough in the brilliant-hued leaves of autumn to care for gathering them; the leaves of the former grow in clusters of threes, and those of the latter in fives. As somebody has suggested in a juvenile story book, every child should be taught to associate the five leaves in a cluster with the fingers on the human hand, and given to understand that when these numbers agree they can be brought into contact with perfect safety. It may spare our readers no little suffering to bear this point in mind during their October rambles in the fields.

Setting Fence Posts

◆ ◆ ◆ ◆ ◆

From THE CULTIVATOR, 1845

Posts for fences or other purposes, set into the ground, will last double the length of time by being put into the middle of the hole. The space around the post filled with small stones instead of earth, the earth does not come in contact with the post, and air is also admitted into the hole, both of which probably tend to prevent decay. In constructing fences, the earth taken from the hole is placed directly under the line of the fence, thus forming a ridge which is a saving equal to twelve feet of boards in four lengths of fence. The stones should be raised three or four inches around the post above the surface of the ground. The posts will not be very firm at first, but after standing through one winter their firmness will be much increased, and will continue to increase for several years.

A post and rail fence constructed in this way forty-five years since, in the vicinity of Boston, is now standing, with the exception of one post, and will probably stand a dozen years more.

Garden Hints

Floral Hints

From VICK'S MONTHLY MAGAZINE, 1886

For fixing or holding the surface of embankments of light soils, there is nothing better than the Double Poppy. Scatter the seed over the surface, and it will germinate in a few days, and in two weeks its roots will begin to hold the soil, and will finally interlace, forming a strong net-work.

◆ ◆ ◆ ◆ ◆

From VICK'S MONTHLY MAGAZINE, 1880

In forming a bouquet, every flower should be allowed to assume its natural position as far as possible, and enough of the green leaves retained to give life and naturalness to its appearance, without encroaching on the room required by its neighbors.

We have found, in preparing flowers to be copied upon canvas, that there was no arrangement which could equal that which they naturally and accidentally assumed in gathering them in the garden, and so our invariable rule is to tie them just as we find them in our hand, and place them in the vase.

◆ ◆ ◆ ◆ ◆

From ARTHUR'S HOME MAGAZINE, 1870

If you are troubled with injury to bulbs by field mice during the winter, allow me to suggest what has proved with me a remedy. Formerly I covered my bulbs early in the autumn, before frost, and field mice being abundant in the neighborhood, they seemed as soon as cold weather approached to take shelter among my covering and feed on my bulbs. Now, I leave off the covering until the ground is frozen about an inch in depth, and I guess the mice get tired of waiting and go elsewhere.

Nature's Weather Signs

♦ ♦ ♦ ♦ ♦

From JOHNSON'S DICTIONARY OF GARDENING, 1847

RAIN MAY BE EXPECTED — When the sounds of distant waterfalls, &c., are distinctly heard—When the sun rises pale and sparkling—When the sun rises amidst ruddy clouds—When the sun sets behind a dark cloud—When there is no dew after heat in summer—When there is much hoar frost in winter—When mists rest on the mountain tops—When snails and frogs beset your evening walk—When gnats bite vigorously—When animals are unusually restless.

♦ ♦ ♦ ♦ ♦

FAIR WEATHER MAY BE EXPECTED — When none of the signs of rain just given occur—When the sun sets red and cloudless—When the moon's horns are sharp—When the stars shine brightly—When smoke rises easily—When moths and beetles appear in numbers.

A Home·made Insecticide

◆ ◆ ◆ ◆

From DR. CHASE'S RECEIPT BOOK, 1888

A writer in the *Deutsche-Zeitung* states that he had an opportunity of trying a remedy for destroying green fly and other insects which infest plants. It was not his own discovery, but he found it among other receipts in some provincial paper. The stems and leaves of the tomato are well boiled in hot water, and when the liquor is cold it is syringed over the plants attacked by insects. It destroys black or green fly, caterpillars, etc.; and it leaves behind a peculiar odor which prevents insects from coming again for a time. He states that he found this remedy more effectual than fumigating, washing, etc. Through neglect a house of camelias had become almost hopelessly infested with black lice, but two syringings with tomato plant decoction thoroughly cleansed them.

How to Grow Strawberries on a Small Lot

♦ ♦ ♦ ♦ ♦

From the book HOMEMADE CONTRIVANCES, 1899

Probably many readers have heard of the plan of raising strawberries on the outside of a barrel. If one has only a small city or village lot, or "back yard," the experiment is well worth trying. The accompanying illustration shows one or two wrinkles that may help make the experiment a success. First bore the holes all about the barrel, then put inside a drain pipe made of four strips of board, reaching from the top to the bottom. The joints should not be tight. Now fill in earth about the pipe and set out the strawberry plants in all the holes and over the top. Put the barrel on a bit of plank, on the bottom of which wide casters have been screwed. The barrel can then be turned about every few days to bring the sun to all the plants. An ordinary flour barrel will answer very well for trying this interesting experiment.

How to Plant a Tree

From HARPER'S MONTHLY, 1886

The hole destined to receive a shade or fruit tree should be at least three feet in diameter and two feet deep. It then should be partially filled with good surface soil, upon which the tree should stand, so that its roots could extend naturally according to their original growth. Good fine loam should be sifted through and over them, and they should not be permitted to come in contact with decaying matter of coarse, unfermented manure. The tree should be set as deeply in the soil as it stood when taken up. As the earth is thrown gently through and over the roots it should be packed lightly against them with the foot, and water, should the season be rather dry and warm, poured in from time to time to settle the fine soil about them. The surface should be levelled at last with a slight dip toward the tree, so that spring and summer rains may be retained directly about the roots. Then a mulch of coarse manure is helpful, for it keeps the surface moist, and its richness will reach the roots gradually in a diluted form. A mulch of straw, leaves, or coarse hay is better than none at all. After being planted, three stout stakes should be inserted firmly in the earth at the three points of a triangle, the tree being its center. Then by a rope of straw or some soft material the tree should be braced firmly between the protecting stakes, and thus it is kept from being whipped around by the wind. Should periods of drought ensue during the growing season, it would be well to rake the mulch one side, and saturate the ground around the young tree with an abundance of water, and the mulch afterward spread as before.

Garden Hints

From THE REGISTER OF RURAL AFFAIRS, 1865 and 1866

In order to prolong the flowering season in perpetual and other roses, and in annual and perennial plants, clip off with a pair of scissors the seed-vessels, as soon as the petals fall. This prevents the exhaustion of the plant in the forming of seed, continues its vigor, and preserves a neater appearance of the whole plant. At the same time, the use of the scissors will enable the gardener to impart a symmetrical form to the plants.

◆ ◆ ◆ ◆ ◆

The time will come when the value of fallen leaves, for mulching the ground and protecting tender plants, will be better understood that at present. They impart advantages when used as a mulch, namely, lightness of covering and perfect protection. For covering tender plants they are peculiarly fitted—being always so dry as not to suffocate or rot the plant, and the thin plates of air interposed between them, entirely excluding frost if sufficient depth is given. A late number of the Genesee Farmer mentions the case of a gardener who has had remarkable success with roses, the tender kinds of which he keeps through the winter in open ground by a thorough covering with leaves. When a foot in thickness, with a few branches of evergreens on the top to prevent them from blowing away, no frost can penetrate.

Figure 1

Figure 2

Figure 3

♦ ♦ ♦ ♦ ♦

Good Advice

From THE REGISTER OF RURAL AFFAIRS, 1868

After Trying Various modes for protecting melons and cucumbers from the striped bug and other insects, we find the following superior to any other. Two small twigs of osier or other slender wood, about a foot and a half or two feet long, are bent over the hill of young plants and the ends thrust in the ground, as represented by fig. 1. A newspaper is then placed upon these curved sticks covering the whole, and the edges are fastened down all around by a covering of earth as shown in fig. 2. This constitutes the whole contrivance, and affords complete protection from all insects; the paper being thin and porous, admits a sufficient supply of air and light, at the same time sheltering from cold winds. Plants thus protected have grown twice as fast as those fully exposed. Another advantage of this mode is the protection it affords from night frosts, rendering it admirably adapted to plants which have been early removed from the hot-bed. Lastly and not least, is its cheapness. A gardener will apply it to a dozen hills in as many minutes by the watch, the material costing nothing to any one who takes a political newspaper.

Unless the paper is very thin and fragile, heavy rains will not break it. Strong plants sometimes burst through; but a better way, when they become large, is to tear a hole in the top, as shown in fig. 3, the remaining paper at the sides still affording some protection, although plants of this size are usually safe from injury.

Wild·flowers for the Garden

From ARTHUR'S HOME MAGAZINE, 1870

◆ ◆ ◆ ◆ ◆

The most indifferent admirer of nature cannot but feel a thrill of pleasure at sight of the first flowers of spring. The trailing arbutus, the anemone, the violet, are all favorites; and many look forward to their appearance in early spring with an ardent longing which can only be satisfied by a sight of their fragile, pale, delicate-tinted blossoms.

As soon as spring is here, we find them in the woods and glens, on hillsides and by roadsides, a lavish array of loveliness; while yet our gardens show only hyacinths, snowdrops, narcissus, and other spring-blooming plants, in a waste of yet untenanted flower-beds.

But why should not our wild-flowers be domesticated? Some few of these have been, we know; but there are many more equally deserving. They blossom so early that if transplanted into our beds and borders, we might, from the earliest spring, rejoice in a profusion of bloom, which would continue until the garden flowers were ready to take their places.

It is unnecessary to specify wild-flowers by name. Our desire is simply to prompt our readers to adopt these little children of the woods and fields, and see if they will not repay the love and care bestowed upon them, by even more beautiful and generous bloom than in their wild state. The important thing is to observe the conditions of the plant in its native home—the degree of shade and moisture its nature requires—and supply them as far as possible.

Hints for Autumn

THE LAWN — If Lawn Grass is sown at once, it will have the benefit of the fall showers, and should come up well in a week or so. Give a dressing of manure before hard frosts.

♦ ♦ ♦

PLANTING BULBS — Thousands of people, when they saw the Hyacinths and Tulips in flower last spring, thought that next spring they would have a bed, and hundreds at once sent off orders for bulbs, all in vain. If any one wishes a bed of such flowers next spring, this is the best time to purchase and plant the bulbs.

♦ ♦ ♦

WEEDS — Allowing weeds to ripen their seeds in the garden, late in the season, makes a great deal of trouble for the future.

♦ ♦ ♦

LOOK ABOUT — This fine Autumn weather; look about a little and see what can be done to improve your grounds. Some changes may be desirable, or some trees and bulbs planted. Without forethought there is no garden and no gardener.

The above hints are from VICK'S MONTHLY MAGAZINE, 1880

♦ ♦ ♦ ♦ ♦

Some afternoon when you think everything will be killed with frost at night, pull up your vines that are loaded with green tomatoes and hang them in the cellar; they will ripen off finely. I took some from my cellar last Christmas day, that were very nice.

From THE NEW ENGLAND FARMER, 1858

Test Your Seeds

From the book HOMEMADE CONTRIVANCES, 1899

No one can, by merely looking at them, positively tell whether any particular lot of field, garden, or flower seeds have or have not sufficient vitality of germ to start into vigorous growth. Yet it is a severe loss, often a disastrous one, to go through with all the labor and expense of preparation and planting or sowing, and find too late that the crop is lost because the seeds are defective. All this risk can be saved by a few minutes' time all told, in making a preliminary test, and it should be done before the seed is wanted, and time to get other seed if necessary. Seeds may not have matured the germ; it may have been destroyed by heat or moisture; minute insects may have, unobserved, punctured or eaten out the vital part of a considerable percentage.

Select from the whole mass of the seed, one hundred, or fifty, or even ten seeds, that will be a fair sample of all. For larger seeds, as wheat, corn, oats, peas, etc., take a thin, tough sod, and scatter the counted seeds upon the earth side. Pour upon the seeds another similar sod, earth side down. Set this double sod by the warm side of the house or other building, or of a tight fence, moistening it occasionally as needed. If very cold, cover, or remove to the kitchen or cellar at night. The upper sod can be lifted for observation when desirable. The swelling and starting of the seeds will in a few days, according to the kind, tell what percentage of them will grow—a box of earth will answer instead of sods, both for large and small seeds. Small seeds of vegetables or flowers, and even larger ones, may be put into moist cotton, to be kept slightly moist and placed in the sun or in a light warm room. For small quantities of valuable flower seeds and the like, half a dozen will suffice for a trial test.

A Useful Weed

From the book ALL AROUND THE HOUSE, 1879

◆ ◆ ◆ ◆ ◆

Chicory, "succory," or "wild endive," although it grows wild in our country, is much cultivated abroad. The leaves, unblanched, are bitter, but, soaked some hours in water, the bitter property disappears, and it is used as a salad. When blanched it ranks, with some, among the best winter or spring salads. It is easily raised, and by packing the roots in a trench close together in the fall, and in the early spring laying on some earth well mixed with manure, the young leaves will push out finely blanched, forming a very crisp early salad, much superior, we are told, to the early tough green lettuces. Its growth is rapid, and it can be cut several times in the year; or the roots may be laid in a warm cellar in the fall, away from frost, and the tender leaves will shoot out, nicely blanched, for an excellent winter salad. In Belgium and the Netherlands the roots are scraped, boiled, and used like parsnips.

Save Your Squashes

◆ ◆ ◆ ◆

From DR. CHASE'S RECEIPT BOOK, 1888

The following appeared in the *Southern Husbandman*: "To destroy bugs on squashes and cucumber vines, dissolve a table-spoonful of saltpeter in a pail of water, put a pint of this around each hill, shaping the earth so that it will not spread much, and the thing is done. The more saltpeter, if you can afford it—it is good for vegetable but death to animal life. The bugs burrow in the earth at night and fail to rise in the morning. It is also good to kill grub in peach trees—only use twice as much, say a quart to each tree. There was not a yellow or blistered leaf on 12 or 15 trees to which it was applied last season. No danger of killing any vegetable with it. A concentrated solution applied to beans makes them grow wonderfully."

Figure 1

Figure 2

Figure 3

Scarecrows

From THE AMERICAN AGRICULTURIST, 1878

A ready method of protecting newly-planted fields from crows, or blackbirds, is shown in figure 2. It is made of a light hickory, or other elastic stick, one end of which is stuck into the ground; to the other end is suspended a glass bottle, from which the bottom has been broken off. The cord by which the bottle is suspended passes through the neck; a nail is fastened to this cord to serve as a clapper, and so attached that it will strike the glass when the cord swings. A piece of bright tin, sheet-iron, painted shingle, or slate, is suspended to the end of the cord. When the wind blows, the suspended tin, or other article, is whirled in all directions, and causes the nail to rattle against the glass bottle. The flashing of the bright object, and the bottle, as well as the continued rattle, will keep the birds at a respectable distance, for a time at least. As a variation, which may be used in place of the thin disc, an effective scare-crow may be made thus:— Take a large cork, such as is used in pickle-jars, procure some wing feathers of a goose, chicken, or hawk, and stick these firmly into the cork at three sides, so as to roughly imitate a dilapidated bird. Carve a rough head from a crooked branch, and arrange the tail feathers in an expanded position to catch the wind, by which it is caused to dart hither and thither in a most unexpected manner. This arrangement is shown in figure 3.

Garden Hints
◆ ◆ ◆ ◆ ◆
From THE HORTICULTURIST, 1857

If you want to be successful in transplanting, don't be afraid of working in dull weather. If you are shy of a "Scotch mist," buy an India-rubber macintosh. Nothing is so cruel, to many sorts of trees, as to let their tender fibres patch up in a dry wind, or a bright sun. Such weather may be fun to you, but 'tis death to them.

◆ ◆ ◆

Rhubarb is an invaluable plant to those who like a spring tart. You may have yours ready to cut a week before your neighbor's, without the trouble of forcing, if you set your plants in a border on the south side of a wall or tight board fence, and take the precaution to loosen up the soil, and cover each crown of roots with a bushel basket full of black peat earth the autumn before.

◆ ◆ ◆

When you are planting a tree or shrub, don't be penny-wise and pound-foolish; in other words, so anxious to have it look large, as to be unwilling to cut off a single inch of its top to balance the loss of roots. Remember that if your tree would grow six inches if left "unshortened," it would grow twelve if properly shortened, besides making far healthier shoots and bigger leaves, to say nothing of its being five times as likely not to die.

Plant Small Trees

From THE REGISTER OF RURAL AFFAIRS, 1860

It has been a very general, almost universal desire among tree-planters, to have large-sized trees from the nursery. One person about to set out an orchard, wrote, "Send me *man* trees. I do not want puny little children—but large, full-grown specimens." Another said, "I want the largest trees you have—I don't care much what kind they are—but give me tall ones—if a rod high, all the better." "But," the nurseryman replied, "smaller ones will be better in five years than these." "I don't care, I want big ones; I may not live five years, and I want fruit *now*." Three or four years after, the same planter called again. Without waiting for an inquiry, the nurseryman immediately remarked, "Well, I have some fine large trees which I can furnish." "Don't want 'em! don't want 'em!" was the answer, "I've had enough of large trees—they have cost me ten times as much labor to set out as the small ones I took from necessity. They have not grown one inch; are just the same size I bought them, although I have doctored them and nursed them, and they have borne me only a very few of half-grown worthless fruit. The small trees have already outstripped them, and have begun to bear large, excellent specimens."

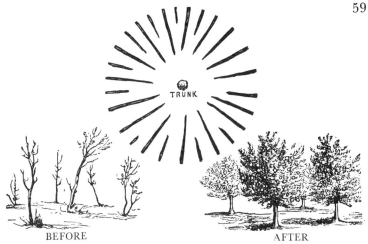

BEFORE   AFTER

Renovate Old Trees
From THE REGISTER OF RURAL AFFAIRS, 1859

When old trees become feeble, there is no better way of imparting to them vigor, than by *manuring*. Instead of adopting the more common practice of digging a circular trench around them and filling this with manure, the operation may be performed in a more perfect and efficient manner by digging narrow radiating trenches from within a few feet of the trunk, directly from it—this will prevent cutting many of the roots. The annexed diagram will show the position of these trenches. These may then be filled with a *compost*, made of turf, stable manure, ashes, and perhaps a little bone manure—the turf to be the chief constituent, say one-half or two-thirds—and the ashes say one-thirtieth. The bone manure is not essential, as its constituent parts are in common manure in small quantities. If this is done in autumn, the roots will be prepared to penetrate it early in spring, and if the tree is not past recovery, it may make a new push. The roots probably extend as far each way as the height of the tree, and the trenches should extend about as far. They need not be cut very near the tree, as the roots are all large there, and would be more likely to be injured and would be little benefitted. The trenches should be only the width of a spade, and may be two to four feet apart.

Plant Evergreens for Protection

From THE REGISTER OF RURAL AFFAIRS, 1866

◆ ◆ ◆ ◆ ◆

Many land-owners, who have a more distinct appreciation of dollars and cents, than of the beauties of nature, cannot see the propriety of occupying ground and labor in setting out ornamental trees. To such, as well as to all others, we wish to urge the importance of planting evergreen trees as a shelter against the cold winds of winter. We once knew a country resident who flanked his house on the sides of prevailing winds with groups and masses of evergreens, from the neighboring forests and borders of swamps—and drew upon himself pretty freely the jeers of his neighbors, for setting out trees that "bore nothing to eat," and were "only good to look at." In the course of years however, when these trees had attained a height of some twenty feet, and had afforded ample shelter from the winds that swept across the bleak hill occupied by his dwelling, the neighbors discovered that the place had become decidedly more comfortable in cold weather—also that many dollars in firewood were annually saved by the beautiful and efficient protection afforded. They began to see new charms in ornamental trees, and were disposed to adopt what they had once ridiculed.

Garden Hints

From PARK'S FLORAL MAGAZINE, 1889, 1890 and 1892

◆ ◆ ◆ ◆ ◆

TIN CANS FOR APPLYING WATER AND LIQUID MANURE — I use Tin Cans with a hole made in the centre of the bottom, in applying water and liquid manure to such plants as Roses, Dahlias and Chrysanthemums. Place the can under the foliage of the plant, so that it will be hidden as much as possible, and sink it into the soil an inch or two. Into this pour the water, or liquid manure. By the cans being sunk into the soil, the contents will slowly penetrate to the roots of the plant, and not flow away over the surface and be lost. ◆ ◆ ◆

BUYING ROSES — Those who wish to purchase Roses for beds or out-door planting should delay their orders till in April. There is nothing gained by obtaining the plants too early. Sometimes they are chilled in transportation, and often they are subject to changes to temperature after received which destroys their vitality and results in their death.

◆ ◆ ◆

A NEW FERTILIZER — I learned of something new and will pass it along. After boiling potatoes for dinner take the water in which they boiled, dilute it a little and put on your Rex Begonias. How they will grow! It is also good for other plants.

A Living Screen Wall

✦ ✦ ◆ ✦ ✦

From THE AMERICAN AGRICULTURIST, 1878

The best screen whether for shutting out the view, or for the shelter it affords, is a living one of evergreen trees. This, however, can not be had at once—time is required to produce it, and while this is growing some other may be supplied. Mr. I. D. Snook, of Yates Co., N.Y., sends us a design for a screen, which may be used as a permanent one, or to serve until one of evergreens has reached high enough to take its place. This, shown in the engraving, has posts, 7 or 8 feet high, which are connected by a cap-piece of boards, cut as there shown, and strands of galvanized iron wire, are passed from post to post, every 12 or 18 inches, according to the kind of plant to be used. One of the best plants for such a screen is a rampant growing grape-vine, such as the "Clinton," or "Taylor," and until this gets established, some annuals, such as Morning-glories, or such quick-growing plants as the Maderia-vine may be used.

An Early Start for Seeds

◆ ◆ ◆ ◆

From the book HOMEMADE CONTRIVANCES, 1899

The ground is often cold when the seed is put into the garden plot. To get the earliest vegetables. have a few boxes without bottoms and with a sliding pane of glass for a top, as shown in the cut. Let the top slope toward the sun. Shut the slide entirely until the plant breaks ground, then ventilate as one would in a hotbed, as suggested in the right-hand sketch. A few such boxes will make some of the garden products ten days earlier—worth trying for.

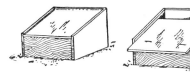

How Birds Help

From THE NATIONAL FARMER'S & HOUSEKEEPER'S CYCLOPEDIA, 1888

The swallow, swift, and hawk are the guardians of the atmosphere. They check the increase of insects that otherwise would overload it. Woodpeckers, creepers, and chickadees are the guardians of the trunks of trees. Warblers and flycatchers protect the foliage. Blackbirds, crows, thrushes, and larks protect the surface of the soil. Snipe and woodcock protect the soil under the surface. Each tribe has its respective duties to perform in the economy of nature, and it is an undoubted fact that if the birds were all swept off the face of the earth man could not live upon it, vegetation would wither and die; insects would become so numerous that no living being could withstand their attacks. The wholesale destruction occasioned by grasshoppers which have devastated the West is to a great extent, perhaps, caused by the thinning out of the birds, such as grouse, prairie hens, etc., which feed upon them. The great and inestimable service done to the farmer, gardener, and florist by the birds is only becoming known by sad experience. Spare the birds and save the fruit; the little corn and fruit taken by them is more than compensated by the quantities of noxious insects they destroy. The long-persecuted crow has been found by actual experience to do more good by the vast quantities of grubs and insects he devours than the harm he does in the grains of corn he pulls up. He is, after all, rather a friend than an enemy to the farmer.

How to Lay·out Curved Garden Beds

From THE REGISTER OF RURAL AFFAIRS, 1877

Arabesque beds, require an accurate eye for designing them in the best manner; but a graceful and curved outline may be preserved by the use of a rope, the mode of working with which we here describe:

If small figures are to be laid out, the rope may be of moderate size, so as to make short curves; for large figures a larger and stiffer rope may be used. The operator places it upon the ground, and forms with it the outline of the proposed figure. Then, before beginning work, insert a few small pegs or stakes barely touching it. These will keep it at its place while the sharp spade is inserted all along its side in cutting out the bed.

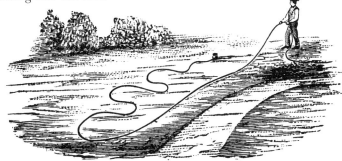

How to Face Your Flowers

From THE REGISTER OF RURAL AFFAIRS, 1855

◆ ◆ ◆ ◆ ◆

It often happens that two different flower beds may be equally well managed and flourish alike, yet one may be a mass of brilliancy while the other exhibits little or no beauty. There are many flowers which always face the light of the sun; consequently the beds should be so placed that the spectator in the walk or window, should look them *full in the face.* That is, the strongest light and the position of the spectator should always be on the same side of the bed. This will be found particularly necessary with the pansy or tri-colored violet, and some other of the smaller flowering plants.

A Garden Toad

From THE CULTIVATOR, 1844

In proportion to what he is capable of doing, there is not a more useful animal to man than the toad. He has not bad habits, and in the pursuit of a livelihood he is sure to benefit some body.

The spawn of the toad, like that of the frog, is deposited in the water. As soon as the young have attained the use of their legs, they take to the land, and subsist on such flies, beetles, and worms, as they are able to swallow—thus in obtaining their subsistence, rendering a very essential service to the farmer and gardener. The number of insects in this way destroyed, is immense. As many as fifteen beetles have been found in the stomach of a single toad. It feeds mostly in the night, at which time insects are abroad. It is quite amusing to see the toad seize its prey. In the dusk of evening, it may be seen through the summer season, near the places most frequented by insects, snapping up, almost with the quickness of lightning, every bug or worm that makes its appearance.

Garden Hints

From THE REGISTER OF RURAL AFFAIRS, 1865

HOW TO KEEP GRASS FROM GROWING IN WALKS — When the soil has not been excavated, where the walk is made, to the depth of ten or twelve inches, and the excavation is not filled with stone, gravel, old mortar and other substances, the grass roots on each side of such walks will frequently run into the soil in the walk, and send up shoots so numerous that the walk will be quite green.

Make a weak brine and sprinkle the walks, by means of a water sprinkler, as often as the grass appears. A few pounds of salt used in this way will save a vast amount of hard hoeing, and, at the same time, keep such walks clean and neat.

◆ ◆ ◆ ◆ ◆

HEDGES FOR THE SHADE — A friend inquires what the best hedge plants are to grow in the shade of trees. Nothing is better than the hemlock or the Norway spruce. Any one can readily determine before hand what plants will succeed best, by examining the interior of thickly growing bushes. If, on turning up the branches, the leaves are found dense and healthy inside, such trees will grow well in the shade; but if the inside leaves are dead, or the shoots bare of foliage, they will not succeed. A buckthorn hedge, for example, is found to have all the leaves outside, and none at all toward the centre; as a necessary consequence, the buckthorn is one of the worst of all hedges under the shade of trees.

The Color of Garden Fences

♦ ♦ ♦ ♦ ♦

From THE AMERICAN AGRICULTURIST, 1867

Whitewashed or White Painted Garden fences may be neat and attractive in themselves, but for that reason they are unsuitable. Any surrounding of this kind, that draws attention from the living plants, is as impertinent as a gaudy bonnet over a pretty face. Carpentry and horticulture should not painfully strive for mastery. Green, drab, or other unattractive color, is suitable, and not abominable; white not to be mentioned. The same idea applies to poles, trellises, etc., used for supports, and to the still greater absurdity of whitewashing the trunks of trees. A tallow candle is a poor model to follow in trying to improve the looks of one of the most harmoniously beautiful of nature's productions.

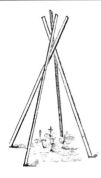

A Cheap Plant Support

Here is an exceedingly cheap and practical substitute for poles and trellis to support climbing plants and vines, and enclose a photograph of it herewith. For four hills it takes four lath or strips, or poles, of the desired length, and two shingle nails. It saves the setting of the poles, lighter and more slender stuff is available, it can be put up after the plant begins to run, it is adjustable to any distance between hills, and needs to be set in the ground only deep enough to prevent slipping; it offers very little resistance to wind, and the vines hold it in place after they begin to climb. The vines form a hollow pyramid, produce more pods or fruit, with better facilities for growth and maturity, than when trained on single poles. The mode of construction is to place two pieces, say of lath, together even, at the end intended for the base, and drive a nail through them against a clincher, two to six inches from the top. Repeat with as many pairs as you want. Let these spread from row to row, and let every two pairs from hill to hill meet in the cross at top. A string, or bit of small wire may be needed to keep the tops in place. When the vines begin to overtop the pyramid, a cross piece may connect pairs of pyramids in the direction of the row by simply resting in the forks of the cross, and the runners be trained to meet, if extent of vine is desired.

Another way is to take three laths or poles and two nails, and make a tripod. This can be spread to two hills in one row and one in the other, in alternation. This last is cheapest, and for low training is probably best. Cross-stretchers, by pairs in rows, of these trios, can also be used, and will render tying at the tops needless. For hops or grapes, or smaller garden or floral climbers, this device is available.

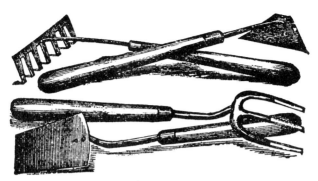

Garden Hints

◆ ◆ ◆ ◆ ◆

From THE REGISTER OF RURAL AFFAIRS, 1858

HANDLES of pruning knives and all other implements that are liable to be lost should be painted of a bright red. The handles of knives and other small tools are usually of a color so near that of the soil, or that of the branches of trees and vines, that it is not easy to find them, if carelessly misplaced.

◆ ◆ ◆

SEEDS OF WILD PLANTS — Those who wish to introduce the early flowering wild plants into their grounds, should look out for seeds as soon as they ripen, and if it is desirable to remove the roots, put a mark of some kind near the plant, so that it will be seen when the foliage is dead.

◆ ◆ ◆ ◆ ◆

From THE NATIONAL FARMER'S & HOUSEKEEPER'S CYCLOPEDIA, 1888

PROTECT THE SWALLOW — Among insectivorous birds the swallow is worthy of great encouragement. An examination of the stomachs of eighteen swallows killed at different seasons of the year showed that they contained an average of 406 undigested insects each, and not a single grain of corn (of any kind), or the least particle of fruit or a trace of any vegetable.

Rocks in the Garden

From VICK'S MONTHLY MAGAZINE, 1886

One good use of stones in the garden is in layering, for we find that shoots and branches of all plants, shrubs and trees root much more quickly if placed in the soil and covered with a large stone than if pegged down in the usual way. Even for many hardy plants we find this plan of stone-layering very successful. A few good boulders half sunk in the turf make a fine position for clumps of Yucca flaccide, or of Acanthus, or, if carefully grouped and fringed with any small-leaved, creeping forms of Ivy, they make very beautiful groups, and add variety to flat surfaces.

◆ ◆ ◆ ◆ ◆

The action of frost is well known in splitting rocks, and it is often employed in quarrying stone. This is accomplished by drilling several holes in a line across the surface which it is desired to crack, filling them with water and letting frost do the rest of the work.

Another plan not unfrequently employed, is to drill similar holes and driving pieces of wood into them that exactly fit the holes, breaking off the sticks close to the surface, to pour water upon them so that the sticks may swell by absorbing water. This force is often sufficient to crack large rocks.

From THE HOMESTEAD, 1858

Weeding

From VICK'S MONTHLY MAGAZINE, 1886

◆ ◆ ◆ ◆ ◆

All small, delicate crops which require hand weeding should be cleaned out at once as soon as they can be seen in the row. A delay of forty-eight hours will often double the work, and a week may entirely ruin the crop. The best time to destroy a weed is before it comes up, and the mere stirring of the surface for an inch as soon as the land is dry enough to work after a rain will kill nine-tenths of the weeds that have started. Make it a rule that a weed shall never go to seed on your garden. The average farmer's garden of one-fourth of an acre ripens enough weed seed to supply the entire farm, and it will take more than five years to get such a garden clean, but if clean cultivation is persevered the time will come when the labor of cultivating the garden will be reduced one-half. It is not difficult to keep a garden clear of weeds if all the crops are planted in rows running the length of the garden.

Decorate With Vines

From VICK'S MONTHLY MAGAZINE, 1886

Beautiful effects can be produced by the judicious planting and training of hardy climbing plants about the house, and with especial reference to the ornamentation of entrance porches and verandas, and this feature of ornamental gardening should receive more general attention than is given to it. It can be done without the aid of the professional gardener, though we should, by all means, have his assistance, if possible, for the trained mind and the skilled hand are as capable of exhibiting their superiority in garden work as in any other art. But, even without such assistance, one who appreciates beauty and loves nature cannot fail with such materials as thrify-growing and gracefully climbing and trailing plants, to produce effects that are pleasing to the eye.

◆ ◆ ◆ ◆ ◆

I have a pretty summer house. It is composed entirely of lilacs, white Persian and Common, planted to form a square. They were planted more than ten years ago, and are now over twenty feet high, and although there is no roof the branches meet so much over head that the sun can only come in a little at mid-day. When the lilacs are in bloom it is lovely.

From a letter to PARK'S FLORAL MAGAZINE, 1892

Take Care of Your Lawn
◆ ◆ ◆ ◆

From VICK'S MONTHLY MAGAZINE, 1886

Fix a long handle to a sharp chisel and thrust it into the soil by the side of a Dandelion plant, and cut it off below the surface. In most cases they will not start again. Some weeds are very tenacious of life, and a common one of this kind is the Burdock. Having its head cut off does not seem to prevent its starting again. We have found a good way to manage this plant by cutting it off just below the surface of the ground, removing the top part, and then pouring a few drops of kerosene oil on the cut surface of the root; it appears to penetrate and destroy it wholly.

◆ ◆ ◆

Ants can be trapped with pieces of coarse sponge sprinkled with sugar. Place the bits of sponge near the ant holes, and visit them several times a day, picking them up quickly and dropping them into a pail of water carried along for the purpose. Persistence in this course for a short time will clear them away. We have seen limewater advised to destroy ants by pouring it in their runways, and also a solution of common washing soda in the same manner, but have had no experience with either of them.

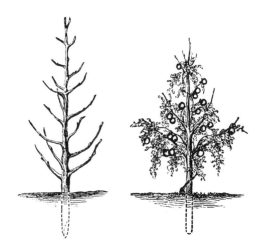

Kitchen Garden Hints

From THE REGISTER OF RURAL AFFAIRS, 1858

TOMATO TREES — Short, thick, spreading bushes, sharpened and put into the ground by first making a hole with a crowbar, serve as an admirable support for the stems of the tomato plant, which, when loaded with its fruit among the spreading branches of the bushes, look like dwarf trees in full bearing.

♦ ♦ ♦ ♦ ♦

GARDEN ROTATION — The following enumeration of the different families of garden vegetables will enable the gardener to plan a rotation, so that similar plants will not occupy the same soil in successive years—those classed together should not succeed each other.

1. Peas, beans.
2. Cabbage, cauliflower, brocoli, turnip, radish.
3. Carrot, parsnip, parsley, celery.
4. Potato, tomato, egg plant.
5. Cucumber, melon gourd, squash.
6. Lettuce, salsify, endive, chicory.
7. Onion, garlic, shallot, leek.

Don't Get Sunstroke

From THE AMERICAN AGRICULTURIST, 1878

It is said that a soldier hired himself to a farmer to dig his early potatoes; after a hearty breakfast, on a hot August morning, the new help seated himself in the shade of the barn, saying to the farmer, "Now, if you want your potatoes dug, bring them along."---We can not all dig our potatoes in the shade, but there is much exposure to our intense mid-summer heat, that may be, and should be avoided, not only as a matter of comfort, but of health. Sunstrokes are more frequently heard of in cities, as there every casualty of the kind goes at once into the papers, while the same percentage of sunstrokes, in a population scattered over a county or two, would scarcely be heard of. We often see a kind-hearted farmer arrange a shade for his horse, while he forgets himself. Of course, most of the active work must be done under full exposure of the sun, or at least with only the protection afforded by the broad brim of a straw hat. He must be deficient in ingenuity, who can not "conjure up" some screen which shall break the force of the sun, upon the head, at least.

Put Winter to Work in Your Garden

From THE CULTIVATOR, 1845

♦ ♦ ♦ ♦ ♦

Few are aware of the beneficial effects upon all kinds of soil, and especially upon heavy land, of a thorough freezing and thawing. Eight cubic feet of water in freezing, swells to nine feet at least. Soils filled with water expand in the same way. The water dispersed all through the pores when freezing, cracks and pulverizes the soil, and fits it for plants, and releases much plant food. This freezing also kills many insects, insect eggs, and weed seeds. It is wise, then to plow fields and spade the gardens into ridges and furrows in Autumn, so as to let the frost down as deeply as possible. This can be done at any time before the ground becomes solid. If so wet that it packs, the freezing will lighten it up again. The operation pays well. If ground be left in ridges with deep dead furrows or ditches, it will drain and dry off, and become warm a week or two earlier in spring, which is an important gain for the cultivator at that season.

The Garden in Winter

◆ ◆ ◆ ◆ ◆

From VICK'S MONTHLY MAGAZINE, 1881

Every true gardener loves his garden all the year round. He prepares it carefully for the time when it becomes a memory and a hope; and it is not without attraction to him even in the bare aspects of winter. In New England it is necessary, not only to clear up the rubbish and leave a neat looking garden for the winter, but to protect many of the shrubs from the cold, the wind, and the alternate freezing and thawing which assail them, more or less, for five months of the year. We lately saw one which we enjoyed looking at, although the ice and snow lay all about it. The Rhododendrons, Altheas, some of the Roses, Forsythias, Halesias, the Fringe tree, and various other shrubs were protected by branches of common White Pine, easily procured from the woods, and answering better for the plants than a close covering. These Pine boughs tied around the shrubs were really ornamental, bearing so gracefully the burden of the snow, and waving their green tassels in triumph above it. A little care of this kind can make your gardens pretty to look at in winter, while the cheap protection is far better than the old pieces of matting or carpeting, which disfigure what they guard.

Decorative Gates and Entrances

From ARTHUR'S HOME MAGAZINE, 1870

Arbors covered with flowering vines are very pretty, and so are arches over entrances and gateways. These are not necessarily expensive, but can be made by any one who can handle a hatchet, a hammer, and a spade, and when completed they will vie in elegance and beauty with those of far more pretending construction.

There is nothing prettier than rustic work, and this any one can accomplish. Two beanpoles placed one each side of a gateway, and united at the top by a discarded barrel-hoop, or by cross-pieces of shorter poles, make an excellent framework for morning-glories to run upon. The same design carried still further, and made to form six or eight sides, and almost any of the climbers trained over it, will become a beautiful summer house.

A single pole with strings set out some three or four feet from its base, and fastened at the top of the pole, the strings furnishing support for Cyprus vine, scarlet runner, nasturtium, or any of the climbers, makes a fine pyramid of bloom, and will form a striking centre for a flower-garden.

How to Grow a Lawn on a Hill

♦ ♦ ♦ ♦ ♦

From the book GARDENING FOR PLEASURE, 1888

It is exceedingly difficult to get a growth of grass from seed on a sloping bank at an angle of even fifteen degrees, because a heavy shower of rain on the sloping bank would wash off the fresh soil before the grass seed has formed enough roots to hold the young grass in place. To remedy this, the following plan will be found most effective. To an area fifteen by twenty—three hundred square feet—or in this proportion, be the area large or small, take two quarts of lawn grass seed and mix it with four bushels of rather stiff soil, to which add two bushels of cow manure*; mix the whole with water to the consistency of thin mortar. This mixture is to be spread on the sloping bank, first having scratched the surface of the bank with a rake. It should be spread as thinly as will make a smooth and even surface; in short, just as plaster is spread on a wall. The grass seed will start rapidly, and quickly make a sod of the richest green, its smooth, hard surface preventing its being furrowed out by the rains. It will be necessary, until the grass has fully covered the surface, to keep the plastered bank covered with hay or straw to prevent the covering from drying or cracking.

♦ ♦ ♦ ♦ ♦

*This is a rough, barn manure with hay as a prime ingredient.
If you don't keep a cow, a mixture of grass clippings, peat moss
and commercial fertilizer should work as well.

Drive Pests Away

From DR. CHASE'S RECEIPT BOOK, 1888

AGAINST MOSQUITOES — If mosquitoes or other bloodsuckers infest our sleeping rooms at night, we uncork a bottle of the oil of pennyroyal*, and these animals leave in great haste, nor will they return so long as the room is loaded with the fumes of that aromatic herb.

♦ ♦ ♦

RATS, TO DRIVE AWAY — If rats enter the cellar, a little powdered potash thrown in their holes, or mixed with meal and scattered in their runways, never fails to drive them away.

♦ ♦ ♦

ROACHES, ANTS, ETC., TO KEEP FROM THE BUTTERY — Cayenne pepper will keep the buttery and store room free from ants and cockroaches. If a mouse makes an entrance into any part of your dwelling, saturate a rag with cayenne, in solution, and stuff it into the hole, which can then be repaired with either wood or mortar. No mouse or rat will cut that rag for the purpose of opening communication with a depot of supplies.

*If oil of Pennyroyal can't be found, a strong extract
of any other Mint should work as well.

Household Hints

Hints on Putting·up Fruit

From THE NATIONAL FARMER'S & HOUSEKEEPER'S CYCLOPEDIA, 1888

FASTENING FRUIT JARS — Very many housekeepers are greatly annoyed by the opening of their fruit jars after they have been carefully sealed. The difficulty arises from the fact that the rubber bands furnished with them are so hard, have so little rubber in them, that they do not yield to compression, and hence do not become tight. Boiling the bands before using is said to obviate the difficulty.

MOLD ON JELLY — If the paper which is put over jelly be dipped in the white of an egg, it will when dry be tight and firm, and keep the fruit from molding with much more certainty than if it is dipped in alcohol or brandy. The paper which is laid next the fruit is meant, not that which is tied or pasted over the glass.

BOTTLING FRUIT — Have ready some dry glass bottles, wide-mouthed and clean. Burn a match in each to exhaust the air; place the fruit quickly in each; cork with soft bungs or corks, and put in a cool oven; let them remain until the fruit has shrunken one-fourth. Take out the bottles; heat the corks well in and cover them with melted rosin. If the fruit has been picked dry, and is quite sound, it will keep for months in a cool, dry place, and retain all the flavor.

Good Advice

◆ ◆ ◆ ◆ ◆

Never leave any vegetables soaking in water. It destroys the real flavor. Potatoes are often peeled and left soaking in water some time before using. This is a very bad practice. They, like all kinds of vegetables, should be washed quickly when it is time to put them on to cook, and, without being allowed to remain in the cold water at all, should be at once transferred to the kettle of boiling water in which they are to be cooked. Lettuce is greatly injured by lying in water. Put it on ice when gathered, and wash just before sending to the table. From the book ALL AROUND THE HOUSE, 1879

◆ ◆ ◆

Lemon-juice, thickened with salt, powdered starch, and soft-soap, laid over stains, mildew, or iron-rust, will remove them if the articles are spread on the grass where the sun will strike them. This is sure, and does not injure the fabric.
From THE UNIVERSAL RECEIPT BOOK, 1831

◆ ◆ ◆

To ascertain whether or not water be fit for domestic purposes, to a glassful of the water add a few drops of the solution of soap in alcohol. If the water be pure it will continue limpid, if impure, white flakes will be formed.
From the book ALL AROUND THE HOUSE, 1879

The Bake·Kettle

From THE AMERICAN AGRICULTURIST, 1870

When cooking stoves came in, the bake-kettle, or covered skillet, went out, and with it went a large part of what was good in our American cookery. It is a shallow kettle with a lid, which has a turned-up edge, and upon which coals are placed; and the thing to be cooked is "between two fires." Those who are roughing it in log cabins or in camp, know what a useful thing it is. In it the bread is baked, meat roasted or fried, coffee browned, dishwater heated—in short, it is the one thing handy to have in the house. I say, much good cooking disappeared with the bake-kettle. It allowed food to be cooked as it seldom is by the stove—long-continued, slow cooking, with all the juices and flavors kept in. Were there ever such chicken and veal pies as our mothers used to make in the bake-kettle? We have nowadays what is called roast veal—half burned and wholly spoiled in the stove oven. But stuff a knuckle of veal and put it in the bake-kettle and let it "sizzle" with fire above and below for three or four hours. It cooks quietly and slowly, all the moisture is retained, and comes out not only a delicious, but a digestible morsel.

Fresh Salad in Winter

From THE HOMESTEAD, 1858

❖ ❖ ❖ ❖ ❖

There is a very pretty experiment which we have frequently seen young people interested in, showing very well the
germination of seeds, or the way in which seeds throw out
their roots and stalks. It is this. Take a tumbler with smooth
sides, so that you can see through it clearly, and fill it nearly
full with water; on the water lay some cotton and on the
cotton plant a few seeds. In a few days they will have swelled
and then a little white root will throw itself downward and a
small green shoot will show itself which gradually, day after
day, will grow till they reach quite a large size. Water must be
added frequently as the plants grow.

On the same principle if you take a large plate or platter,
and spread cotton wool or a piece of blanket in it, and sow
lettuce seed, you may raise enough for several dishes of salad.
It should be kept in a warm dark closet till the seeds have
sprouted, and then the water always kept abundantly
supplied. After the seeds have fairly sprouted they should be
brought into the light, and they will soon grow to a mass of
green plants which will be quite ornamental, and if they are
not used for anything else they will in their fresh green looks
repay the little trouble of keeping the dish filled with water.

How Fresh are Your Eggs?

From THE NATIONAL FARMER'S & HOUSEKEEPER'S CYCLOPEDIA, 1888

Fresh eggs, when held to the light, the white will look clear, and the yellow distinct; if not good, they will have a clouded appearance.

When eggs are stale, the white will be thin and watery, and the yolk will not be a uniform color, when broken; if there is no mustiness, or disagreeable smell, eggs in this state are not unfit for making cakes, puddings, etc.

Eggs for boiling should be as fresh as possible; a new laid egg will generally recommend itself, by the delicate transparency of its shell.

◆ ◆ ◆ ◆ ◆

From the book THE HEARTHSTONE, 1887

To determine the exact age of eggs, dissolve about four ounces of common salt in a quart of pure water and then immerse the egg. If it be only a day or so old, it will sink to the bottom of the vessel, but if it be three days old it will float in the liquid; if more than five it comes to the surface, and rises above in proportion to its increased age.

To Keep Flowers Fresh

From ARTHUR'S HOME MAGAZINE, 1870

WHEN A BOUQUET IS RECEIVED, I at once sprinkle it lightly with fresh water, and then put it in a vessel containing soapsuds. This will keep the flowers as freshly as if just gathered. Then every morning take the bouquet out of the suds, and lay it sideway—the stock entering first— into clean water; keep it there a minute or two, then take it out and sprinkle the flowers lightly by the hand with water, replace it in the soapsuds, and it will bloom as fresh as when first gathered. The soapsuds need changing every three or four days. By observing these rules, a bouquet may be kept bright and beautiful for at least a month, and will last still longer in a passable state.

◆ ◆ ◆

TO KEEP FLOWERS FRESH — Put a tablespoonful of powdered charcoal into the water which is to receive the flower stalks. The charcoal will settle immediately in the bottom of the vase, and the water will remain liquid. This done, it is not necessary to renew the water or the charcoal for several days. The flowers will keep their freshness and their perfume, and will look and smell as fine as those just brought in from the garden.

◆ ◆ ◆

KEEPING FLOWERS FRESH — If wilted flowers have about half an inch of their stems cut off, and the stalk thus trimmed inserted into boiling water, they will in a few moments resume almost their original freshness. The process is most applicable to colored flowers, as roses, geraniums, azaleas, &c., white ones turning yellow. Thick-petalled flowers show the most marked improvement.

House Plants

From the book THE AMERICAN WOMAN'S HOME, 1869

The Care of House-Plants is a matter of daily attention, and well repays all labor expended upon it. The soil of house-plants shoud be renewed every year as previously directed. In winter, they should be kept as dry as they can be without wilting. Many house-plants are injured by giving them too much water, when they have little light and fresh air. This makes them grow spindling. The more fresh air, warmth and light they have, the more water is needed. They ought not be be kept very warm in winter, nor exposed to great changes of atmosphere. Forty degrees is a proper temperature for plants in winter, when they have little sun and air. When plants have become spindling, cut off their heads entirely, and cover the pot in the earth, where it has the morning sun only. A new and flourishing head will spring out. Few house-plants can bear the sun at noon. When insects infest plants, set them in a closet or under a barrel, and burn tobacco under them. The smoke kills any insect enveloped in it. When plants are frozen, cold water and a gradual restoration of warmth are the best remedies. Never use very cold water for plants at any season.

Winter Blossoms

◆ ◆ ◆ ◆ ◆

From VICK'S MONTHLY MAGAZINE, 1881

On the fourth day of December last we cut a few branches from our Cherry tree, in the front yard, and set them in a small bottle filled with water; every week or so a little more water was added, to make up the loss by evaporation. By February second we had leaves and flowers in fine display; just one month later than we expected, for we were told, when making the cuttings, that they would bloom in four weeks. They are none the less welcome, however, for having to wait and watch the swelling bud, the small speck of green, the bursting flower, and the unfolding leaf. They give us, at this season of the year, a novel and unique mantel ornament.

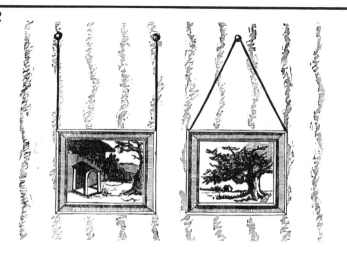

Good Advice

From PRACTICAL HOUSEKEEPING, 1883

TO CLEAN A PAPERED WALL — Cut into eight pieces a large loaf of bread two days old, blow dust off wall with a bellows, rub down with a piece of the bread, in half yard strokes, beginning at the top of the room, until upper part is cleaned, then go round again repeating until all has been gone over. Or, better, take about two quarts of wheat bran, tie it in a bundle of coarse flannel, and rub it over the paper. It will clean the paper nicely. If done carefully, so that every spot is touched, the paper will look almost like new. Dry corn meal may be used instead of bread, applying it with a cloth. If grease spots appear, put blotting paper over spots and press with a hot flat-iron.

◆ ◆ ◆

From ARTHUR'S HOME MAGAZINE, 1870

A room with pictures in it, and a room without pictures, differ by nearly as much as a room with windows and a room without windows. Nothing, we think, is more melancholy, particularly to a person who has to pass much time in his room, than blank walls and nothing on them, for pictures are loop-holes of escape to the soul, leading it to other scenes and other spheres.

Housekeeping Hints

From PRACTICAL HOUSEKEEPING, 1883

TO RENEW STAINED FLOORS—that have grown a little dull, rub thoroughly with beeswax and turpentine. Repeat this whenever they need it.

◆ ◆ ◆

TO CLEAN VARNISHED FURNITURE, there is nothing so good as a woolen rag dampened in spirits of turpentine. This takes all the dust and cloud from carvings and panels. When they have been thoroughly cleaned with the turpentine, go over the surface again with a bit of flannel dipped in linseed oil, rubbing it well into the wood.

◆ ◆ ◆

TO DRIVE NAILS — Nails dipped in soap will drive easily in hard wood.

◆ ◆ ◆

TO KEEP PAINT-BRUSHES — Turn a new brush bristles up, open, pour in a spoonful of good varnish, and keep it in that position until dry, and the bristles will never "shed" in painting. The varnish also keeps it from shrinking and falling to pieces. As soon as a job is finished, wipe brush clean, wrap in piece of paper, and hang it in a small deep vessel containing oil. This will keep painting and varnish brushes clean and ready for use.

Comfortable Chairs
From THE AMERICAN AGRICULTURIST, 1874
◆ ◆ ◆ ◆ ◆

How rarely does one find really comfortable chairs anywhere? People seem to buy the style of furniture in fashion at the time, and this is usually made with a greater regard to show, than to comfort. In the country, where hard working men and women need easy and restful seats, there seems to be a great lack of them. The best room may have some hair-covered or rep-covered rocking or lounging chairs, but these are too good for daily use, by tired people in their working clothes, and as for taking the best furniture out of doors, that is not to be thought of. We Americans, especially those of us who live in the country, make but very little use of our spacious summer parlor—"all out doors" — A wide spreading tree, a vine covered arbor, a broad veranda or porch, and awning like a huge umbrella, or a tent with no sides or even an open shed is a much more comfortable place for sewing, reading, and resting, than any place in-doors, and often comes handy for ironing and other work. For the enjoyment of the open air in any case, seats and chairs that are not too good for rough usage or too rough for ease are needed. The good old-fashioned framed chairs, with split-wood or flagged seats, have long been discarded for the glued work of the modern cabinet maker, but we are glad to see them coming into use again; they were formerly the regular furniture of the farm house; now they are offered as luxuries at the fashionable furnishing stores, and are purchased by those city persons who go into the country for the summer, and wish to take some strong comfortable chairs with them.

Housekeeping Hints

From THE REGISTER OF RURAL AFFAIRS, 1857

TO CLEAN BRASS — Rub the tarnished or rusted brass, by means of a cloth or sponge, with diluted acid, such as the sulphuric, or even with strong vinegar. Afterwards, wash it with hot water, to remove the acid, and finish with dry whiting.* ♦ ♦ ♦

OILING LATCHES AND HINGES — Every person who lives in a house, should spend fifteen minutes once every month in going over every part with a teaspoonful of oil and a feather, and give all the hinges, locks and latches a touch. It will save an incredible amount of scraping, banging, jarring, squeaking, harsh grating, dismal creaking, and other divers and several noises, which result from the want of a little oil.

♦ ♦ ♦

MARBLE FIREPLACES AND TABLES — Never wash them with soap suds— the potash of the soap decomposes the carbonate of lime, and in time destroys the polish.

♦ ♦ ♦

DOOR KNOBS — To secure the paint around them in cleaning, place a piece of pasteboard with a hole cut to encircle them, and a slit to slip on.

♦ ♦ ♦

GILT FRAMES, if cleaned, are soon worn and spoiled—to prevent which, preserve them by applying a transparent varnish.

*Fine chalk powder

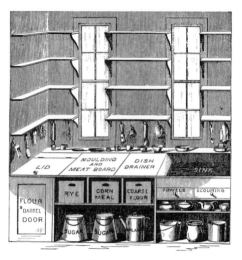

Kitchen Hints

From THE NATIONAL FARMER'S & HOUSEKEEPER'S CYCLOPEDIA, 1888

USE OF LEMON LEAVES — Lemon seeds, if planted and treated as house plants, will make pretty little shrubs. The leaves can then be used for flavoring. Tie a few in a cloth and drop in apple sauce when boiling and nearly done. It is a cheap essence.

♦ ♦ ♦

UNPLEASANT ODOR FROM CABBAGE — The reason why cabbage emits such a disagreeable smell when boiling is because the process dissolves the essential oil. The water should be changed when the cabbage is half-boiled, and it will thus acquire a greater sweetness.

♦ ♦ ♦

TO BEAT EGGS QUICKLY — To beat the whites of eggs quickly put in a pinch of salt. The cooler the eggs the quicker they will froth. Salt cools and also freshens them.

♦ ♦ ♦ ♦ ♦

GRIDDLE CAKES — To prevent them from sticking, rub salt over the griddle with a piece of bread before greasing.

From THE REGISTER OF RURAL AFFAIRS, 1857

Laundry Hints

From PRACTICAL HOUSEKEEPING, 1883

♦ ♦ ♦

TO TAKE OUT PAINT — Equal parts of ammonia and spirits of turpentine will take paint out of clothing, no matter how dry or hard it may be. Saturate the spot two or three times and then wash out in soap-suds.

TAKE OUT MACHINE OIL — Rub with a little lard or butter and wash in warm water and soap, or, simply rub first with a little soap and wash out in cold water.

TO REMOVE INK STAINS FROM CLOTHING — Dip the spots in pure melted tallow; wash out the tallow and the ink will come out. If articles are rubbed out in cold water while the stain is fresh, the stain will often be entirely removed.

TO TAKE GREASE OUT OF SILKS, WOOLENS, PAPER, FLOORS, ETC. — Grate thick over the spot French (or common will do) chalk, cover with brown paper, set on it a hot flatiron, and let it remain until cool; repeat if necessary. The iron must not be so hot as to burn paper or cloth.

TO STIFFEN LINEN CUFFS AND COLLARS — Add a small piece of white wax and one tea-spoon brandy to a pint of fine starch. In ironing, if the iron sticks, soap the bottom of it.

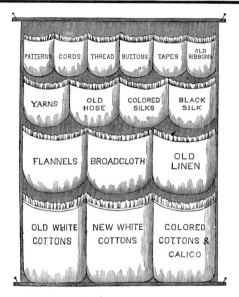

A Useful Contrivance

From the book THE AMERICAN WOMAN'S HOME, 1869

The figure above is a very great labor and space-saving invention. It is made of calico, and fastened to the side of a closet or a door, to hold all the bundles that are usually stowed in trunks and drawers. India rubber or elastic tape drawn into hems to hold the contents of the bag is better than tape-strings. Each bag should be labeled with the name of its contents, written with indelible ink on white tape sewed on to the bag. Such systematic arrangement saves much time and annoyance. Drawers or trunks to hold these articles can not be kept so easily on good order, and moreoever, occupy spaces saved by this contrivance.

◆ ◆ ◆ ◆ ◆

From the book THE HEARTHSTONE, 1887

To render pencil marks indelible, take well-skimmed milk, and dilute with an equal bulk of water. Wash the pencil marks, whether writing or drawing, with this liquid, using a soft flat camel-hair brush, and avoid all rubbing. Place upon a flat board to dry.

Laundry Hints

♦ ♦ ♦ ♦ ♦

From THE REGISTER OF RURAL AFFAIRS, 1857

TO WASH SILK WITH GREAT SUCCESS, spread it on a table, and then rub it with a sponge dipped in a mixture of equal parts of soft soap, brandy and cane molasses. Rinse it thoroughly in three successive portions of water, and iron it before quite dry.

♦ ♦ ♦

TO PREVENT COLORS FADING — Dip new calico, pocket-handkerchiefs, etc., in salt water.

♦ ♦ ♦

GLOSS ON LINEN — To restore the gloss commonly observed on newly purchased collars and shirt bosoms, add a spoonful of gum-arabic water to a pint of the starch as usually made for this purpose. Two ounces of clear gum-arabic may be dissolved in a pint of water, and after standing overnight, may be racked off, and kept in a bottle ready for use.

♦ ♦ ♦

MOTHS are effectually excluded from clothes kept in cedar chests, or with cedar shingles occasionally laid between the clothes, in wardrobes, closets, etc.

Kitchen Hints

From THE NATIONAL FARMER'S & HOUSEKEEPER'S CYCLOPEDIA, 1888

In washing dishes, fill a dish-pan half full of very hot water, and put to the quantity a half cup of milk. It softens the hardest water, gives the dishes a clear, bright look, and preserves the hands from the rough skin or "chapping" which comes from the use of soap. It cleans the greasiest dishes without leaving the water covered with a greasy scum. Iron pots, saucepans, and dishes of any kind in which food is cooked, should be filled in part with hot water and set on the range as soon as the food is removed, to be kept hot till ready to wash them. This sends most of the grease from the pan into the hot water. As soon as ready to wash these pots and kettles, pour out the hot, greasy water, and wash in very hot milk and water, as above directed.

◆ ◆ ◆

From the book THE HEARTHSTONE, 1887

CLEANING KETTLES — Throw a shovelful of wood-ashes into the pan, pot, or kettle which has been burned; fill with water; let it boil while the dishes are being washed. Then wash it with a coarse cloth; this plan will be found to be a great savings of hands, spoons and temper.

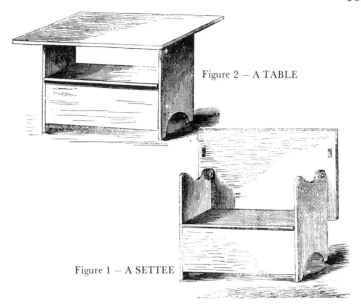

Figure 2 — A TABLE

Figure 1 — A SETTEE

A Useful Piece of Furniture

From THE AMERICAN AGRICULTURIST, 1874

In many rural households, the space allotted to the kitchen is often cramped and narrowed too much. Women are not often consulted when houses are built, and it is usually the kitchen that suffers for lack of room. A piece of kitchen furniture, therefore, that will answer three distinct purposes, is a great convenience. Here is one (figure 1) that is at once a settee, a trunk, and an ironing table or bake board. There is a box or trunk, in which one may stow away many things that usually lie about, having no special place allotted for them otherwise. The lid of this trunk forms the seat of the settee. The ends are raised up, forming the arms. The back of it is pivoted upon one side of the ends, and when it is turned down, as seen in figure 2, it forms a table. When it is turned down, it is held in its place by two small hooks, seen in the illustration at figure 1.

A Cure for the Cold

From PRACTICAL HOUSEKEEPING, 1883

TO CURE A COLD — A bad cold should be "nipped in the bud." To do this no medicine is required. A person who finds he has taken cold should bundle up unusually warm in bed with a bottle of hot water at his feet. The object is to create a mild perspiration the entire night. Before dressing in the morning take sponge bath in cool water and apply friction to the skin until is is in a glow. The cold, probably will then have disappeared, but if not follow the same course another night. But this remedy must be applied promptly after noting the first indications—such as sneezing or running at the nose; if left a day or two, the cold will be sure to run the course. Often toasting the feet the whole evening by the fire will answer the purpose.

◆ ◆ ◆

FOR COLDS, drink hot pennyroyal tea.*

◆ ◆ ◆

CHANGING CLOTHING — People often take cold by removing heavy under-clothing too early in the spring. This should never be done until weather is settled. When about to make the change, take a cold hand-bath or sponge-bath and rub briskly, in the morning, and there is no danger of taking cold.

*Any other mint tea should give comparable results.

Culinary Cures

From the book THE HEARTHSTONE, 1887

◆ ◆ ◆ ◆ ◆

MEDICAL VALUE OF ASPARAGUS — A medical cor-respondent of an English journal says that the advantages of asparagus are not sufficiently appreciated by those who suffer with rheumatism and gout. Slight cases of rheumatism are cured in a few days by feeding on this delicious esculent; and more chronic cases are much relieved, especially if the patient avoids all acids, whether in food or beverage. The Jerusalem artichoke has also a similar effect in relieving rheumatism. The heads may be eaten in the usual way, but tea made from the leaves of the stalk and taken three or four time a day is a certain remedy, though not equally agreeable.

◆ ◆ ◆ ◆ ◆

THE LEMON — Few people know the value of lemon-juice. A piece of lemon bound upon a corn will cure it in a few days; it should be renewed night and morning. A free use of lemon-juice and sugar will always relieve a cough. Most people feel poorly in the spring, but if they would eat a lemon before breakfast every day for a week—with or without sugar, as they like—they would find it better than any medicine.

Take Care of Your Feet

From PRACTICAL HOUSEKEEPING, 1883

RELIEF FOR BURNING FEET — To relieve burning feet, first discard tight boots; then take one pint of bran and one ounce of bicarbonate of soda, put in a foot-bath, add one gallon of hot water; when cool enough, soak your feet in this mixture for fifteen minutes. The relief is instantaneous. This must be repeated every night for a week or perhaps more. The bran and bicarbonate should be made fresh after a week's use. Bicarbonate of soda can be purchased for a small price per pound from wholesale druggists. The burning sensation is produced by the pores of the skin being closed, so that the feet do not perspire.

◆ ◆ ◆

WATER-PROOF SHOES — To make shoes water-proof and make them last a long time, dissolve beeswax and add a little sweet-oil to thin it. Before the shoes are worn, warm the soles and pour the melted wax on with a teaspoon; and then hold it close to the fire till it soaks into the leather; then add more till the leather ceases to absorb it.

◆ ◆ ◆

TO SOFTEN LEATHER — The best oil for making boots and harness leather soft and pliable, is castor-oil.

To Care for Injuries

◆ ◆ ◆ ◆ ◆

From PRACTICAL HOUSEKEEPING, 1883

FOR SPRAINS — The white of an egg, and salt mixed to a thick paste is one of the best remedies for sprains, or bruises, or lameness, for man or beast. Rub well the part affected.

◆ ◆ ◆

SPRAINS — If a sprain is nothing more than a sprain—that is, if no bones are broken or put out—wrap the part in several folds of flannel which has been wrung out of hot water, and cover it with a dry bandage, and rest it for some days, or even weeks. Entire rest at first, and moderate rest afterward, are absolutely necessary after a sprain. If it is in the ankle, the foot should be raised as high as may be comfortable; if in the wrist, it should be carried in a sling.

◆ ◆ ◆

A VALUABLE LINIMENT — One ounce wormwood to one pint alcohol. Or, bruise the green stalks of wormwood, moisten with vinegar, and apply to the sprain. Good for man or beast.

How to Deal with Insects

From PRACTICAL HOUSEKEEPING, 1883

TO KEEP OFF FLIES — Paint walls or rub over picture frames with laurel-oil.

♦ ♦ ♦

BEE STINGS — Any absorbent will give relief from bee stings, but perhaps nothing is more effectual than lean raw meat. The sting of a bee or wasp may be almost instantly relieved by it.

♦ ♦ ♦

STINGS OF INSECTS — Are relieved by the application of ammonia, or common table salt, well rubbed in, or a slice of an onion, to the part.

♦ ♦ ♦

BRANCHES OF THE ELDER-BUSH—hung in the dining-room of a house, will clear the room of flies. There is an odor which the insects detest.

♦ ♦ ♦

RED ANTS — A small bag of sulphur kept in a drawer or cupboard will drive away red ants.

♦ ♦ ♦ ♦ ♦

THE LEAVES of the common walnut-tree, placed over doors, windows, mantels, or in wreaths or bunches about the house, will drive flies away.

From the book THE HEARTHSTONE, 1887

Good Advice

From THE NATIONAL FARMER'S & HOUSEKEEPER'S CYCLOPEDIA, 1888

DRIVING NAILS INTO HARD WOOD — The editor of an agricultural periodical witnessed an experiment of driving nails into hard seasoned timber, fairly dried. He says that the first two nails, after passing through a pine board, entered about one inch, and then doubled down under the hammer; but on dipping the points of the other six or eight nails into lard, every one was driven home with the least difficulty. Carpenters who are engaged in repairing old buildings sometimes carry a small lump of lard or tallow for this purpose on one of their boots or shoes.

♦ ♦ ♦

TO REMOVE A SCREW RUSTED IN THE WOOD — Heat a poker in the fire red-hot, and put it on top of a screw for minute or two; then take the screw-driver, and you will easily get it out, if you do it whilst it is warm.

♦ ♦ ♦

TO PREVENT RUST — A composition that will effectually prevent iron, steel, etc., from rusting. Mix with varnish four-fifths of well rectified spirits of turpentine. Apply this varnish with a sponge, and the articles will retain their metallic brilliancy, and not be liable to rust.

Market Hints

From PRACTICAL HOUSEKEEPING, 1883

When buying Beef, select that which is of a cherry-red color after a fresh cut has been for a few moments exposed to air. The fat should be of a light straw color, and the meat marbled throughout with fat. High-colored, coarse-grained beef, with the fat a deep yellow, should be rejected. In corn-fed beef the fat is yellowish, while that fattened on grasses is whiter.

The best Fowls are fat, plump, with skin nearly white, and the grain of the flesh fine. Old fowls have long, thin necks and feet, and the flesh on the legs and back has a purplish shade.

When fresh, the eyes of Fish are full and bright, and the gills a fine clear red, the body stiff, and the smell not unpleasant. Lobsters, when freshly caught, have some muscular action in their claws which may be exited by pressing the eyes. When Scallops and Hard-shell Clams are fresh, the shell closes tight. Oysters, if alive and healthy, close tight upon the knife.

Grocery Hints

From PRACTICAL HOUSEKEEPING, 1883

ALL VEGETABLES snap crisply when fresh; if they bend and present a wilted appearance, they are stale. If wilted, they can be partly restored by being sprinkled with water, and laid in a cool, dark place.

♦ ♦ ♦

CAULIFLOWERS are best when large, solid and creamy. When stale the leaves are wilted and show dark spots.

♦ ♦ ♦

POTATOES — Select those of medium size, smooth, with small eyes. To test, cut off a piece of the large end; if spotted, they are unsound. In the spring, when potatoes are beginning to sprout, place a basket of them in a tub, pour *boiling* water over them; in a moment or two take out and place in sun to dry (on the grass is a good place), and then return to cellar. If they have sprouted too much it is best to first rub them off.

♦ ♦ ♦

CELERY stalks should be white, solid and clean. Celery begins in August, but it is better and sweeter after frost.

Kitchen Hints
From PRACTICAL HOUSEKEEPING, 1883

ONION ODORS — When cooking onions, set a tin-cup of vinegar on the stove and let it boil, and it is said you will smell no disagreeable odor.

◆

ALL KINDS OF HERBS — Gather on a dry day, just before or while in blossom, tie in bundles, blossom downward. When perfectly dry, wrap the medicinal ones in paper, and keep from air. Pick off the leaves of those to be used in cooking, pound, sift them fine, and cork up tightly in bottles.

◆

AN EASY WAY TO CLEAN SILVER ARTICLES — Set fire to some wheat-straw, collect the ashes, and, after powdering it, sift it through muslin. Polish the silver plate with a little of it, applied to some soft leather.

◆

DISH-WATER AND SOAP-SUDS—poured about the roots of young fruit-trees, currant and raspberry bushes, etc., facilitate their growth.

◆

WORTH KNOWING — To purify a room of unpleasant odors, burn vinegar, resin, or sugar; in using hard water for dish-water add a little milk; to clean paint, add to two quarts hot water, two table-spoons turpentine and one of skimmed milk, and only soap enough to make suds, and it will clean and give luster; iron rust on marble can generally be removed with lemon-juice; a thin coat of varnish applied to straw-matting makes it more durable and adds to its beauty.

The Homestead Calendar
of work in its' season

Spring. Summer.

Autumn. Winter.

From
THE AMERICAN AGRICULTURIST, from 1866 to 1880

January

The amount of out-of-door work which can be done this month will depend upon the mildness of severity of the season. One main point, however, should be constantly in mind, and it is that whatever is done now will facilitate the spring work.

BUILDINGS.—Desirable alterations and new erections may be discussed and planned, timber and stones hauled when sledding is good, and preparations completed before the frost begins to come out, immediately after which is the best time to dig cellars, etc., and do grading.

HEDGES.—Prune during mild weather; at the South it can be done at any time during the winter.

GREEN CORD-WOOD should be drawn and put in a pile to season. Do not let it remain in the woods, and then have to draw it in the summer when you should be doing more important work.

LAYING OUT of beds and walls may be planned, and in a mild season some of the work may be done.

YOUNG TREES, from the beginning, need constant supervision. Were the trees properly planted, no stakes will be needed, but if from careless planting or accident, any tree has been thrown out of the perpendicular, straighten it up and tie it to a stake.

February

CLEARING LAND.—This is a very good season in which to blast rocks, cut alders and willows, and often those tussocks of coarse grass, called "bogs." Ditches may be dug in swamps, and such work done.

FIRE-WOOD.—"In peace prepare for war." Though the whole year is before us, trust that no future time will be better to cut fire-wood than the present—that is, the winter. Have cord wood piled to shed water to the east.

SAFETY OF BUILDINGS AGAINST FIRE.—To secure this, examine chimneys and flues, for places where smoke may escape, and be sure that sparks cannot. Be constantly careful of combustible bodies, and of lights. Allow no smoking, or uncovered lights in or near the barns.

TOOLS are to be overhauled and repaired, and those needed made or purchased. A home-made roller, marker, reel for a garden-line and the like, are great helps, even in a small garden.

WRITE DOWN everything you have to do during the next four or five months; and then see if there is not something that you can do now that will save time and labor.

At the South, in favorable localities, hot-beds may be started, and Lettuce, Radishes and Cabbages sown in them, and the half hardy vegetables, such as Beets, Carrots, Turnips, etc., sown in the open ground, and the early sorts of Potatoes planted.

March

There is no month of all the twelve, for which it is more difficult to write these Notes, than March. It is on the border between winter and spring, and while in the northernmost localities winter still lingers, our readers in the Middle and Southern States are fairly in the midst of their spring work. As in other months our Notes are a little in advance of the season, as it is very easy for the reader to look back, should he find what we have indicated for March is with him practicable only for April. Those who have neglected to order trees, plants, seeds, etc., until now, should lose no time in procuring their supplies.

CLUMPS OF PERENNIAL plants that have been in place for several years may be taken up, divided, and reset in fresh soil. Paeonies and a few others should only be disturbed in autumn.

INJURED TREES should be looked to at once. If limbs have been broken by accumulations of snow and ice, make a smooth wound and cover it with melted grafting wax or thick paint.

NEW LAWNS should have the soil thoroughly prepared and well enriched. Our experience in sowing mixed seeds has not been satisfactory. For a rich, and especially a lime-stone soil, we should sow Kentucky Blue Grass, and for light sandy soils, Red-top, or that variety of it known as "Rhode Island Bent," with, perhaps, a quart of White Clover Seed to each bushed of grass-seed.

SMALL PLOTS AND MARGINS OF LAWNS are best laid with sod. In sodding a plot, make the soil thoroughly fertile, and take care that there are no loose places that will settle.

April

THE LAWN.—In case grass must be sown, or wait until next fall, prepare the soil thoroughly, and sow either Kentucky Blue Grass, Red-Top, or that variety of it called R. I. Bent, with about a quart of white clover to the bushel. On rich soil three, and on poor five bushels to the acre will be needed. Divide into two or three parcels, sowing each in a different direction. Roll well. Cultivators differ as to the utility of sowing oats with the grass seed; at this late season it will be well to sow a quart of oats with each bushel of seed, as the oat plants will then not be too thick, and will afford a much needed shade to the young grass. In making a new lawn, if possible, sod the margins next the roads, flower-beds, etc. If the plot is small and turf can be procured, sod the whole; lay it with care, and pat or pound it down well. Old lawns and those sown early will need mowing, and for this a

LAWN MOWER is indispensable, on even a small place. Where there are so many good machines, we cannot advise one in preference to another. The machine should be used every 8 or 10 days, according to the growth; when mowed often the clippings may be left on the grass. Annual seeds will disappear before frequent mowing.

PERENNIAL WEEDS must be dug, pulled, or cut. Cutting with a knife or spud just below the surface will kill most of them. The English put a few drops of oil or vitriol in the heart of each plantain or other large weed. We have not tried it.

RAINY DAYS may be employed in cleaning tools, implements, and machines, and putting them in good order for work when they will be wanted.

May

Impatience is the great fault of all lovers of flowers; from the boy or girl who plants seeds one day and digs them up the next, to the older one who has read all about gardening and has invested untold sums in plants, all are impatient. Those who have, despite our frequent caution not to be in a hurry, put out their verbenas, heliotropes and the like, and have seen what work these cold May storms have made with them, will probably recollect that these plants are raised in a warm propagating house, and that the change is a little too severe. We do not advise, in the climate of New York, the putting out of any of these things before the 20th of May, and the first of June is full soon enough, as that time the soil gets warm, the cold nights are over, and the plants have only to go on and grow. If put out too early they get a chill, from which they are a long while in recovering.

ANNUALS may be sown; the labels upon the seed-packages usually state whether the plants will bear transplanting, or must be sown in place.

CLIMBERS are useful for shade, for decorating verandas, and for making a screen to hide unsightly objects. Where the woody kinds can not be waited for, annuals may be used with good effect. Canary Vine, Thunbergias, Cobaea, Maurandias and other are all good, and some of the finer Morning Glories, though the flowers are short-lived, are very showy.

LARGE WEEDS in lawns, can only be eradicated by weeding; if the plantains, dandelions, docks, etc., appear, pull them in a moist time, or cut well below the surface with a knife. Annual weeds soon give way to frequent mowing, and die without seeding.

FREQUENT MOWING before hot weather sets in, will help thicken the turf.

June

The most important crop to be looked after this month is weeds. A sharp steel rake or a hoe-rake should be kept in constant use, and in a properly managed garden no weed will get so large that it cannot be demolished by the use of one of these. It takes but little time to go over the garden with a rake, and if it be frequently done, it will save much subsequent digging with the hoe.

ANNUALS will need transplanting, and those sowed where they are to bloom are to be thinned. Crowding is a common fault with those who grow annuals, and we seldom see a well developed specimen. Seeds of many sorts may still be sown.

BEDDING PLANTS.—Ageratums, Gazaniass, Verbenas, etc., may be made much more effective if they are pegged down, so as to best cover the surface. This is especially necessary in windy places.

BULBS should have all the time they require for leaf-growth, and not be lifted until the leaves show signs of decay. When taken up, let the bulbs dry off and the leaves thoroughly wither before they are removed. Wrap the bulbs in paper, label, and store in a cool place, free from vermin.

NEATNESS of a garden is in good measure through the agency of sticks and strings. Plants that need support should be kept tied up, but the means by which the effect is produced should be, as much as possible, concealed. Under head of neatness is included the care of gravel and other walks, frequent mowing of lawns, keeping edging in trim, etc.

WEEDS.—We end these notes as we began, with the injunction to never let a weed get too large to be raked out. Don't raise any weed seed.

July

July should have been called the Month of Weeds. The larger share of the cultivator's energy, in whatever department, is expended in keeping down the plants that are not wanted. Those who claim that weeds are a great blessing, as they induce a frequent stirring of the soil, can now enjoy this blessing in the fullest abundance. Weeds, like fire, are easily controlled, if attacked while small, but when they get fairly established, it is often cheaper to plow up the crop, then to undertake to weed it.

ANNUALS.—Quick growing sorts may be sown now for late flowering.

CLIMBERS.—Keep neatly disposed upon the trellises, and provide supports for all such as need them.

GRAPE VINES.—The laterals will now be pushing vigorously. Pinch their growth back to one leaf. Do not let young vines overbear. One bunch to the shoot is sufficient. Keep all vines, young or old, tied up to a stake or trellis, and keep off all volunteer shoots.

LAWNS require frequent cutting to keep the grass looking fresh and velvety; this will also kill annual weeds. Perennial weeds must be taken out when young, with a spud.

PERENNIALS.—Keep the ground carefully weeded. Sow seeds as fast as they ripen; most kinds will make plants strong enough to winter safely, and bloom next year. Some will remain dormant until spring.

BEDS.—Save seeds of forest trees and shrubs, as fast as ripe. Most kinds need to be preserved in sand, to prevent them from becoming too dry.

August

Work now begins to tell. The weeds, which it seemed almost impossible to conquer during the rainy spring, now die after being uprooted, instead of saucily putting up their heads the next day, as if in gratitude for being transplanted by the hoeing.

LAWNS must be mowed frequently, and the machine should be in operation once a week. This frequent mowing will allow the clippings to be left on the ground as a mulch, and as they decay, as a manure, and thus save much top-dressing.

MEADOWS AND PASTURES will be greatly benefited by a light dressing of artificial manure. 100 pounds of nitrate of soda, with a bushel of finely ground gypsum, per acre, will work a great change for the better.

PROPAGATION from cuttings is easily done in a close shaded frame placed on sandy soil. A frame covered with cloth will answer if one has no hot-bed frame and sash. Many shrubs, taken just as the wood is hardening, and most soft-wooded plants, will strike readily in a frame like this. Unless one has the means for keeping the tender kinds of plants over the winter in good condition, it is better to buy bedding plants each spring.

SEEDS.—Save always from the best flowers. Sow perennials and biennials as soon as ripe. Cut away all spent flower clusters if seeds are not wanted.

THE SWAMPS are now dry, and work on them should not be neglected. Getting out muck for use in the winter, and digging ditches, can be better done in August than at any other time.

YOUNG TREES require a mulch at this time to protect them from drying out at the roots.

September

There is a great deal of work to be done in September, but it is not all of that driving, hurrying kind like much of the summer and spring work.

BRUSH.—If there are any brush or large weeds in or around the garden, they should be cut and burned now, and the ashes applied to the land.

LAWNS.—Mow often to keep the annual weeds from flowering and seeding. Sow grass seed in any bare spots, so that it may have the benefit of the autumn rains.

NEW LAWNS may be made and the grass seed sown this month. Fall sowing is preferred to that in spring if the season is favorable for its getting a good start before winter comes.

ORNAMENTAL TREES AND SHRUBS may often be advantageously transplanted in Autumn. Many prefer this season for the removal of Evergreens; success with these depends quite as much upon HOW as upon WHEN it is done, the greatest care to prevent drying of the roots being essential at any season.

PERENNIALS AND BIENNIALS.—Sow seeds this month in well prepared beds, and keep well weeded.

PRESERVING fruit, either by drying or canning, is to be attended to as the different sorts ripen. A drying house of some kind is useful where the quantity is large. Fruit dried out-of-doors should be covered by some open fabric to keep off flies and other insects.

WEEDS.—Mow or pull while in bloom or before; if possible, use as an ingredient of compost heaps. If seeds have formed, dry the weeds, burn them, and use the ashes.

October

If any improvements are designed in the grounds around the house, new walks or drives to be laid out, now is a favorable time to make them, and much better than in spring when the rush and hurry of work is on. If the ground does not lie so that there is a natural drainage, lay underdrains.

BUILDINGS.—A little labor upon them now will tell. A board here and a nail there, and a few shingles newly set, will save many dollars' worth of loss or expense later in the season, when storms and winds do their work.

HOUSE PLANTS.—Remove to the house at once such plants as it is desirable to save for another season. Cut back both root and branch, and keep in the shade for a few days, until well established. Make cuttings of all such as it is desirable to propagate.

LAWNS may be laid down this month. Draining, deep plowing, and thorough pulverizing of the soil, should be attended to. Roll after seeding, and just before the ground freezes, roll again.

PERENNIALS.—Even the hardiest do all the better with a winter covering. Divide and re-set clumps.

SPRING BULBS should be planted as soon as they can be had from the dealers. Those who are not fanciers, but wish a general effect, without regard to names, can buy assorted Hyacinths, Tulips, etc., by the dozen, of the dealer's selection, much cheaper than named kinds. Double Tulips are very showy, they make a blaze of color, and are deserving of more attention than they receive.

BULB BEDS need a light, open, and very rich soil; the general rule is to put the bulbs below the surface to a depth equal to their own thickness.

November

A favorable November will give the gardener an opportunity to prepare himself properly for the winter, by clearing up his grounds, plowing, carting manure, and doing many little jobs for which he can not spare the time in early spring. Many hints for October are applicable whenever the ground does not freeze so hard that it can not be worked.

EDGINGS.—Cut and trim neatly all the grass margins bordering the paths and drives, before freezing weather, and protect places where careless drivers are likely to encroach, by driving down stakes.

LAWNS.—It is now too late to sow seed with any prospect of success, but preparations can be made for sowing early in the spring, by leveling the ground, manuring, etc.

TOOLS AND WOODEN APPLIANCES.—See that everything is in perfect order for cold weather. Never allow any implement which can be used another year to remain out of doors. Bean poles, if properly cared for, will last for several seasons, and save considerable time and expense every season. It is the little items which are to be carefully looked after, and it is only by prompt attention to these that success is attained. Don't think that because a roller is wholly of iron that it will not do any harm to leave it out all winter, or because a marker is easily made, that it can be easily replaced, and that the weather will not affect it.

TRELLISES are repaired, or new ones made, more conveniently now than in spring. Use the most durable wood. Chestnut is durable in some soils, red cedar lasts well; locust is the most durable, and where this is scarce, pieces three feet long may be set two and a half feet in the ground and uprights of pine or other lumber spiked to them.

December

Plowing, stump pulling, wall-laying, field-clearing of stones and roots, underdraining, etc., must cease when the thermometer drops down towards zero. Still these are the appropriate labors of those favored sections where the plow may run in every month of the year, and where white clover and annual grasses afford abundant pasturage, though often cropped, from November to May.

The amount of out of door work will depend upon the weather. If the ground is not frozen hard, it will benefit stiff soils to throw them up in ridges, that they may receive the ameliorating influences of the frost. Clean up all rubbish; lay drains if the season permits, and do everything that will save a day's work in spring.

EVERGREENS, as well as dense clumps of shrubbery and evergreen hedges, not of proper form, are very apt to get bent out of shape if not broken down by heavy accumulations of snow. Such accidents should be prevented by removing the snow while it is still light and can be readily shaken off.

EVERGREEN BOUGHS, especially those of the red cedar, may be placed over low shrubs to protect them.

LAWNS should have a good top dressing of rich compost.

PROTECTION must be given to many tender shrubs. Where the case admits of it, laying down and covering with earth is the readiest as well as one of the best ways. Half hardy Roses, Clematises, Wistarias, (in very cold places,) and the like, winter nicely under a covering of earth, provided the spot is so well drained that water cannot settle about them.

Good Reading

♦ ♦ ◆ ♦ ♦

THE ARCHITECTURE OF COUNTRY HOUSES, by A. J. Downing, a reprint of the 1850 original, 484p, softcover, $7.95 + 85¢ p&h — Dover Publications, 31 East Second St., Mineola, NY 11501

COTTAGE RESIDENCES, by A.J. Downing, a reprint of the 1842 original, 352p, softcover, $6.95 + 85¢ p&h — Dover Publications, 31 East Second St., Mineola, NY 11501

COUNTRY ARCHITECTURE, by Lawrence Grow, 100 original, 19th century plans, for barns, stables, gazebos, greenhouses, smokehouses, sheds and other outbuildings, 128 p, softcover, $9.95 + 1.50 p&h — The Main Street Press, William Case House, Pittstown, NY 08867

BEAUTIFYING COUNTRY HOMES, by Jacob Weidenmann, a reprint of the original 1870 landscape guide, 108p, softcover, $9.95 + 2.00 p&h — American Life Foundation, Box 349, Watkins Glen, NY 14891

BACK TO BASICS, How to Learn and Enjoy Traditional American Skills, edited by Norman Mack, 456p, hardcover — Reader's Digest, Pleasantville, New York

THE BACKYARD HOMESTEAD, MINI FARM & GARDEN LOG BOOK, by John Jeavons, J. Morgodor Griffin & Robin Leler, a record book, calendar and guide to an efficient homestead, 224p, softcover, $8.95 + 1.00 p&h — Ten Speed Press, Box 7123, Berkeley, CA 94707

THE COUNTRY GARDENERS ALMANAC, by Martin Lawrence, a complete calendar of gardening chores with practical advice culled from 19th century farm journals, 224p, softcover, $9.95 + 1.50 p&h — The Main Street Press, William Case House, Pittstown, NJ 08867

COUNTRY PATTERNS, A Sampler of 19th Century American Home and Landscape Design, edited by Donald J. Berg, 128 p, softcover, $8.95 + 1.50 p&h — The Main Street Press, William Case House, Pittstown, NJ 08867

COUNTRY WISDOM, an Almanac of Weather Signs, Moon Lore, Rural Remedies, Fishing and Hunting Facts, Country Recipes, Rules of Thumb & Advice on Mother Nature's Methods, by Jerry Mack Johnson, 154p, hardcover, $6.95 + 1.50 p&h — Jerry Mack Johnson, Box 5200, San Angelo, TX 76902

COUNTRY WISDOM BULLETINS, ninety-seven different, 32p booklets with practical how-to advice on home energy, food gardening, maintenance, cooking, preserving and old-time crafts — Storey Communications, Schoolhouse Road, Pownal, VT 05261

THE FORGOTTEN ARTS SERIES, five books that explain how to master dozens of old-time household skills — Yankee Inc., Box F, Depot Square, Peterborough, NH 03458

HOW TO BUILD IN THE COUNTRY, Good Advice from the Past on How to Choose a Site, Plan, Design, Build, Landscape & Furnish Your Home in the Country, edited by Donald J. Berg, 128p, softcover, $6.95 + 1.00 p&h — Ten Speed Press, Box 7123, Berkeley, CA 94707

MRS. WELCH's COOK BOOK, a reprint of the 1884 original, 288p, softcover, $11.95 + 2.00 p&h — American Life Foundation, Box 349, Watkins Glen, NY 14891

THE VEGETABLE GARDEN, by MM. Vilmorin-Andrieux, a reprint of the 1885 original, 620p, softcover, $11.95 + 1.00 p&h — Ten Speed Press, Box 7123, Berkeley, CA 94707

INDEX

♦ ♦ ♦ ♦ ♦

Donald Berg, an architect, lives with his wife, Christine, and three children in a rapidly running-down 1918 colonial in Rockville Centre, New York. Summers are spent in their country cottage in Vermont where he attempts to grow a variety of vegetables and fruits. His column, HOMESTEAD HINTS, appears in newspapers across the country.